The SIOP® Model for Administrators

Deborah J. Short

Center for Applied Linguistics, Washington, DC

Academic Language Research & Training, Arlington, VA

MaryEllen Vogt

California State University, Long Beach

Jana Echevarría

California State University, Long Beach

PEARSON

Boston   New York   San Francisco
Mexico City   Montreal   Toronto   London   Madrid   Munich   Paris
Hong Kong   Singapore   Tokyo   Cape Town   Sydney

*To Teashie and Vi, for their independent spirits, their support,
and their interest in the work.*
DJS

To Keith, a former elementary school principal whom I have long admired.
MEV

To the REV family.
JE

Executive Editor: Aurora Martínez Ramos
Editorial Assistant: Kara Kikel
Director of Professional Development:
  Alison Maloney
Marketing Manager: Danaë April
Production Editor: Gregory Erb
Editorial Production Service:
  Nesbitt Graphics, Inc.

Composition Buyer: Linda Cox
Manufacturing Buyer: Linda Morris
Electronic Composition:
  Nesbitt Graphics, Inc.
Interior Design: Nesbitt Graphics, Inc.
Photo Researcher: Annie Pickert
Cover Designer: Kristina Mose-Libon

Library of Congress Cataloging-in-Publication Data
Short, Deborah.
  The SIOP® model for administrators/Deborah J. Short, MaryEllen Vogt, Jana Echevarria.
    p. cm.
  Includes bibliographical references and index.
  ISBN-13: 978-0-205-57860-3
  ISBN-10: 0-205-57860-8
  1. English language—Study and teaching—Foreign speakers. 2. Second language
  acquisition—Study and teaching. I. Vogt, MaryEllen. II. Echevarria, Jana, 1956- III. Title.

PE1128.A2S566 2008
42'.0071—dc22   2007044064
Printed in the United States of America

Photo Credits: pages 3, 79: Ellen B. Senisi; p. 17: David Young-Wolff/PhotoEdit; p. 31: Eric
Fowke/PhotoEdit; pages 43, 47, 52, 55, 57, 75: Bob Daemmrich/The Image Works;
p. 63: David Lassman/Syracuse Newspapers/The Image Works. All other photos appear
courtesy of the authors.

10 9 8 7 6 5 4 3 2 1 EDW 12   11   10   09   08

Allyn & Bacon
is an imprint of

PEARSON

www.pearsonhighered.com

ISBN-10: 0-205-57860-8
ISBN-13: 978-0-205-57860-3

contents

As the population of English learners continues to grow rapidly in schools and districts across the United States, administrators need to gain a robust understanding of these learners' academic and language development needs in order to plan and deliver the best programs and instruction for their educational success. We have designed this book to help. Research on the SIOP® Model was conducted in the context of school reform and the instructional framework that resulted from the research has been proven to help English learners develop academic literacy.

Our goal with this book is to provide administrators with background information about educating English learners and specifically address implementation of the SIOP® Model. We hope this book will help administrators be effective instructional leaders in schools with these students. It is worrisome that only 46% of teachers in the 1999–2000 school year reported that "My principal talks to me frequently about my instructional practices" on a U.S. Department of Education national survey (Snyder, Dillow, & Hoffman, 2007). We want to offer administrators the knowledge and tools to dialogue effectively with their teachers about the progress and achievement of English learners.

Over the past decade, we have worked with administrators and teachers on implementing the SIOP® Model in schools and districts throughout the United States. Some have been very large, urban districts with significant numbers of English learners (ELs) and considerable resources. Other districts have been smaller, rural or suburban, with few English learners, bilingual educators, or ESL specialists. Quite a few have seen a rapid increase in ELs and have not had programs in place or teachers trained to work with these students, particularly in the content areas. Although the contexts have varied considerably, issues related to the implementation of the SIOP® Model of sheltered instruction have been remarkably similar. Moreover, the SIOP® Model has been successful in these diverse sites.

This resource was created for the unique roles administrators play—to assist you in efficiently and effectively implementing instructional programs for English learners in your school or program and provide you with practical information to share with others in your district. It is one of a series of books on the SIOP® Model designed to help content and language teachers, coaches, educational specialists, and now administrators plan and deliver the best possible instruction that will significantly increase English learners' academic achievement.

Overview of the Chapters

The first two chapters focus on English learners—their academic performance, their diverse backgrounds, and how individual, cultural, and societal factors have an impact on the speed and ease with which they might learn academic English, a new language. The next chapter describes the SIOP® Model and explains past and recent research studies that show its effectiveness as an instructional approach for ELs. The fourth and fifth chapters delve deeply into the implementation process. You will find recommendations to help you plan for and support SIOP® Model implementation and to restructure a school or program for excellence using the SIOP® Model as the overarching frame. The final chapter closes the book with answers to frequently asked questions about the SIOP® Model, staff development, classroom implementation, program design, and so on.

As you read through the chapters, you will see that each opens with a graphic organizer and content and language objectives for the reader. The use of such objectives and visual aids are hallmarks of the SIOP® Model and we want to help you become accustomed to them and expect to see them when you visit the classrooms of SIOP® teachers. We also have included insights, suggestions, and resources from other administrators who have been using the SIOP® Model at their sites for several years. Their experiences have been invaluable to us in writing this book. We end each chapter with some questions to help you reflect on the information and apply it to your own situation.

In the appendices you will find the Sheltered Instruction Observation Protocol (SIOP®) in both the comprehensive and abbreviated versions. Although we recommend that the rating scale on these instruments be used by trained raters, we would like you to become familiar with the indicators associated with each of the thirty features. In this way you will be better able to determine how well a lesson is meeting the SIOP® Model.

You will find some other useful tools in the appendices. For observations, we offer a SIOP® Model checklist on which you can indicate if a feature is highly evident, somewhat evident, or not evident. We have also provided an action planning form to help you set the course for SIOP® Model implementation.

The book concludes with a glossary of terms related to the instruction of English learners and the process of second language acquisition.

Over the many years of working with teachers and administrators who are implementing the SIOP® Model, we have learned that it is a process that can take from one to three years, or more, depending on the number of educators and schools involved. During the implementation process, teachers and administrators alike have come to realize and appreciate the potential and talents of the English learners in their charge. We welcome you as you begin this journey and hope that you, too, will refine your administrative skills as you assist teachers and other staff to refine their teaching.

Acknowledgments

We are grateful to the following educators who shared their ideas, suggestions, and stories with us over the past few years. Their contributions have enriched this book: Melissa Castillo, Alvaro Hernandez, Wanda Holbrook, Debbie Hutson, Maggie Kerns, Janina Kusielewicz, David McNeil, Kathy Meads, Kendra Moreno, Jennifer Lupold Pearsall, Dr. Michael Rice, Lisa Roberts, Joan Rolston, Marilyn Sanchez, John Seidlitz, Nicole Teyechea, Martha Trejo, and Liz Warner. For those administrators who have already brought the SIOP® Model into their schools and districts, we appreciate your vision and all the efforts you have undertaken to promote effective teaching and learning for English learners.

We also want to acknowledge the critical support and assistance of our editor, Aurora Martínez Ramos, and her enthusiastic staff at Allyn & Bacon. Thanks go to our reviewers as well for their insightful feedback: Kevin Bushman, White Pine School; Susan J. Dean, Southwest Independent School District; and Jennifer Pearsall, Charlotte-Mecklenburg Schools.

Getting to Know English Learners

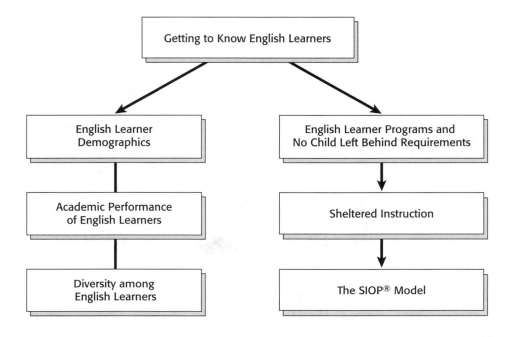

Objectives

After reading, discussing, and reflecting on this chapter, you will be able to meet the following content and language objectives.

Content Objective:

Administrators will compare demographic and achievement data related to English learners with data in their own districts or schools.

Language Objective:

Administrators will describe the diverse English learners in their districts or schools.

In the early 1990s, a small town in central Nebraska opened a meat-packing plant. At the start of that school year there were five students in the district learning English as a new language. The next year, there were more than twenty. In the following school year, the numbers were even higher. Most of the teachers in this district had never taught a second language learner before. Few had any educational background or coursework in the area. Due to a new industry, the student population landscape shifted and the administrators realized they needed to act quickly to prepare the school system to serve these students appropriately. New efforts for professional development were initiated, new curricula and instructional materials were sought or designed, and an English as a second language program was established.

Does this vignette sound like changes that took place in your district over the past decade? Did you have a slow and steady increase of English learners, a rapid influx, or have you had a stable population? Who are the English learners in your school or district, and how have their enrollment numbers changed in the past ten to fifteen years? Have they entered your schools better prepared for the demands of the academic work or less prepared? Do they come to school literate in their first language? In English?

If you work in a district like many, many others, you have seen major changes in the past fifteen years or so and you have been working hard to develop appropriate curricula, hire certified ESL teachers, train other staff to work with English learners, assess these students accurately, meet benchmarks required in the No Child Left Behind Act, and more. You are not alone in facing this challenge. Most English learners enroll in an educational system where they must study and be tested on grade-level curricula in English at the same time they are learning this new language. It is not only difficult for the students but also for their teachers, few of whom have had specific professional development on effective approaches for teaching content to students who are not proficient in the language of instruction. Administrators too confront challenges to design and implement effective programs and assessments for these learners.

English Learner Demographics

The number of English learners (ELs) in our schools continues to grow, and the rate of growth outpaces that of native English-speaking students. Look at Figures 1.1 and 1.2. Figure 1.2 clearly indicates the exponential rise in terms of EL enrollment vis-à-vis total enrollment in K–12 schools. Limited English proficient students (another term for ELs) now comprise 10.5 percent of the nation's total pre-K–12 school enrollment, up from 5 percent in 1990 (Hoffman & Sable, 2006). Based on data reported to the U.S. Department of Education, identified limited English proficient students numbered around 5.1 million in 2004–2005 (NCELA, 2007). The number is likely higher, perhaps doubled, when we

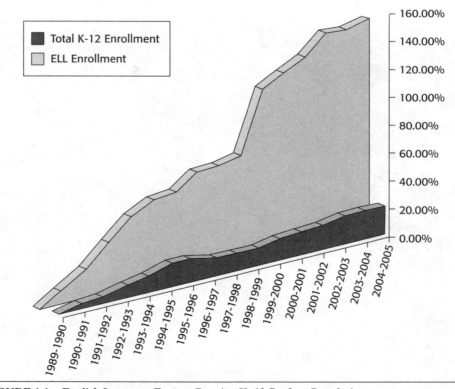

FIGURE 1.1 *English Learners: Fastest-Growing K–12 Student Population*
Source: National Clearinghouse for English Language Acquisition (NCELA).

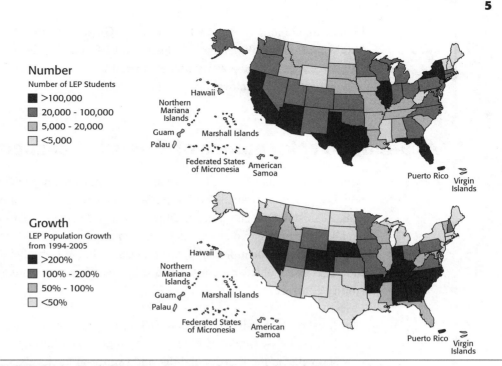

FIGURE 1.2 *English Learner State Population and Growth Rate*

Source: National Clearinghouse for English Language Acquisition (NCELA).

consider students who are still developing proficiency in *academic* English. The increases in EL enrollment will continue over the next several decades, so we need to be prepared to address these students' language and academic needs.

Figure 1.2 reveals that the traditional immigration states, such as California and New York, are no longer the ones that are experiencing rapid growth in the population of English learners (Capps et al., 2005). On the one hand, although they still have the most English learners in terms of absolute enrollment numbers, as the map on the top of Figure 1.2 shows, they are also the states that have well-established programs and curricula and schools of education that prepare teachers to work with linguistically and culturally different students.

On the other hand, changes in the geographic distribution of ELs, as shown in the map on the bottom of Figure 1.2, present new, significant challenges to the numerous districts that have not served these students in the past. North Carolina, for example, experienced a 500 percent growth in their EL student population between 1993 and 2003. Nebraska, Colorado, Nevada, Oregon, Georgia, and Indiana all had more than 200 percent increases in that time period (Batalova, Fix, & Murray, 2005). Many districts in these states have had to start English as a second language (ESL) and bilingual programs from scratch without adequate personnel, program design, or other resources.

Not all of our English learners are recent immigrants. Fifty-seven percent of ELs in Grades 6–12, for example, were born in the United States (Batalova, Fix, & Murray, 2005). The fact that large numbers of second- and third-generation limited English proficient adolescents are not proficient in English by secondary school indicates that many LEP children are not learning the language well even after many years in U.S. schools. The reason for this situation is complex and involves educational, social, economic, and familial issues. Improving programs in schools may help, but it is not the only factor involved. Poverty level, for example, is a key predictor of school success. Poorer students, in general, are less academically successful (Glick & White, 2004), and according to the 2000 U.S. Census, 59 percent of adolescent LEP students live in families with incomes 185 percent below the poverty line compared with 28 percent of adolescents in English-only households (Batalova, Fix, & Murray, 2005).

Academic Performance of English Learners

Although students learning English as a new language are growing in numbers, they are not, as a group, very successful in our schools. Compared to native English speakers or Caucasian students, culturally and linguistically diverse students demonstrate a significant achievement gap on state, national, and international assessments (California Department of Education, 2004; Grigg, Daane, Jin, & Campbell, 2003; Kindler, 2002; Siegel, 2002). Consider the following statistics. How do the students under your responsibility compare?

- Most of the English learners in U.S. schools are of Hispanic descent, and recent National Assessment of Educational Progress (NAEP) tests of reading and writing show that at the fourth-, eighth-, and twelfth-grade levels many more Hispanics performed at the Below Basic level than Whites and Asian/Pacific Islanders and that far fewer performed at Proficient or Advanced levels than those groups (National Center for Education Statistics, 2002).

- Only 4 percent of eighth-grade English learners and 20 percent of students classified as "formerly EL" scored at the proficient or advanced levels on the reading portion of the 2005 NAEP (Perie, Grigg, & Donahue, 2005). This means that 96 percent of the eighth-grade limited English proficient students scored *below* the Basic level. This is particularly noteworthy because NAEP exams often exempt students at the beginning proficiency level of English as a second language (Grigg, Daane, Jin, & Campbell, 2003).

- Only 30 percent of all secondary students read proficiently, but for students of color, the situation is worse: 89 percent of Hispanic students and 86 percent of African-American middle and high school students read below grade level (Perie, Grigg, & Donahue, 2005).

- A recent five-year, statewide evaluation study (Parish et al., 2006) found that English learners with ten years of schooling in California had a less than 40 percent chance of meeting the criteria to be redesignated as fluent English proficient.

- Only 10 percent of young adults who speak English at home fail to complete high school, but the percentage is three times higher (31 percent) for young adult English learners. If ELs reported speaking English with difficulty on the 2000 U.S. Census, their likelihood of completing high school was 18 percent. However, if they reported speaking English very well, their likelihood of graduating was 51 percent (Klein, Bugarin, Beltranena, & McArthur, 2004).

- Since the No Child Left Behind (NCLB) Act has been implemented, there appears to be an increase in the number of high school ELs not receiving a diploma because they failed high-stakes tests, despite fulfilling all other graduation requirements (Biancarosa & Snow, 2004; Edley & Wald, 2002).

● The Center for Education Policy (Kober et al., 2006) reports that ELs have lower pass rates on high school exit exams and lower graduation rates than native speakers, even with test accommodations, such as directions provided in their native language and use of bilingual dictionaries or glossaries.

The achievement gap between English learners and native English speakers is not unexpected nor unexplainable. Second language acquisition is a long-term process, and research has shown that beginning speakers of English need four to seven years of instruction in order to reach the average performance level of their English-speaking peers (Collier, 1987; Cummins, 2006; Thomas & Collier, 2002). Furthermore, the relationship between literacy proficiency and academic achievement grows stronger as grade levels rise—regardless of individual student characteristics. In secondary school classes, language use becomes more complex and more content area specific (Biancarosa & Snow, 2004). Yet under current accountability systems, we test ELs before they are proficient in English. While some states, such as Texas, Illinois, and New Jersey, offer native language assessments in grade-level mathematics and reading (in some languages and at some grade levels), most states require students to take these tests in a language they do not yet know well. Unfortunately, districts and schools are penalized when the students don't perform well.

It is important for administrators to understand that most English learners are studying new, challenging content in and through a language that they do not speak, read, or write proficiently. For ELs to succeed in school, they must master academic literacy, namely the vocabulary, grammar, discussion styles, and genres that are used in different content classes. Using English, ELs, for example, must be able to read and understand expository text, write persuasively, and take notes from lectures. They must articulate their thinking skills in English to make hypotheses, express analyses, and draw conclusions. They must combine their emerging knowledge of English with their knowledge of content topics to complete academic tasks. They must learn *how* to do these tasks, such as explain the steps of a math problem, debate options in cooperative groups, write a laboratory report, and interpret data charts (Echevarria, Vogt, & Short, 2008; Short, 2002). In other words, English learners must develop literacy skills for each content area *in* their second language as they simultaneously learn, comprehend, and apply content area concepts *through* their second language (Garcia & Godina, 2004).

Diversity among English Learners

It is not just enough to know that the enrollment of ELs is growing and these learners experience performance gaps. In order to help our students achieve, we have to know more about their linguistic, educational, and cultural backgrounds. Our English learners are not all the same. They vary in terms of their educational backgrounds, literacy levels in the native language, literacy levels in English, socioeconomic status, cultural norms, and other characteristics. Because they are not a monolithic group, they should not receive the exact same services and educational programs. To the extent possible, we want to consider their backgrounds and then offer appropriate programs and instruction that meet their academic needs and learning goals. Reflect on students in your school or district as you review Figure 1.3 on page 8.

Now consider the following students. They are all English learners and all need some degree of English language development. How far along the path to academic literacy in

FIGURE 1.3 *Diverse Characteristics of English Learners*

Diverse Characteristics of English Learners

First language (L1) background
Educational background
Literacy levels in L1
Literacy levels in English
Entrance age in U.S. schools
Living situation
Culture
Socioeconomic status
Parental education
Expectations for schooling
Life experiences
Mobility

**Think about two students in your school or district.
How do they compare on these characteristics?**

English do you think they have traveled? What type of program would be best for them? How do they compare to the students you are responsible for?

- **Ignacio** was born in Mexico; he came to California at the age of four. He speaks Spanish at home and had limited exposure to English before enrolling in preschool in Long Beach last fall.

- **Muyisa** was born in Zaire, now the Democratic Republic of Congo. She spoke Swahili and Lingala as a child. Her father, a diplomat, was posted at the embassy in Belgium. She went to a French-based international school in Brussels for eight years. Her father was recently assigned to the United Nations in New York City and she has enrolled in a high school with an ESL program there.

- Born in the Dominican Republic, **Diego** came to the United States in third grade. He had attended school in his home town and learned to read and write in Spanish. His family settled in northern New Jersey but they move frequently. He's now in Union City and in a bilingual program.

- **Carlos** attended a Montessori preschool that used English and Spanish. In first grade, he entered a dual language program in Albuquerque, New Mexico. Fifty percent of his day was in Spanish, 50 percent in English. He studied the grade-level curricula throughout elementary school in this way and took state tests in Spanish and in English. In middle school now, he continues with advanced Spanish language arts and literature classes.

- **Elena**, a Russian, enrolled in high school in Beaverton, Oregon, two years ago when her parents, both computer specialists, were recruited by a technology firm nearby. She was an excellent student in St. Petersburg and took advanced science classes and French. At her high school, she takes math and science classes above her grade level, sheltered U.S. history, and content-based ESL classes.

- **Thanh** came from a rural area of Vietnam. Through a family reunification plan, she arrived in the United States at age twelve. She attended school occasionally in her village when she wasn't working in the rice paddies but doesn't read and write Vietnamese well. She will enter a middle school near New Orleans soon.

• **Alejandro** is the son of migrant workers. His family travels around California, following the crops. As a young child, Alejandro went to elementary school in each town they stayed in for various lengths of time, sometimes in an English program, sometimes in a Spanish one. He doesn't read or write well in either language. Now, however, as a young adult, he feels responsible for bringing in income for the family because his father injured his back, so he rarely goes to school anymore.

By reflecting on their varied histories, you might surmise that Muyisa, Carlos, and Elena have the best chance for success in school. They have strong educational backgrounds. Muyisa learned three languages before she started studying English. Carlos is close to becoming proficient in two languages, English and Spanish, due to his dual language program. Elena is handling advanced math and science while learning English. Muyisa and Elena have highly educated parents.

Diego also has a solid educational background that could lead to academic success. He has basic literacy skills in Spanish, and his bilingual program can further his content learning while he learns English. Of concern, however, is the family's mobility. In particular, if they move during the school year, his educational progress could be derailed. Glick & White (2004) found that among adolescents, students with a previous move were twice as likely not to complete high school as those who had not moved.

Students such as Thanh have more difficulty. As older learners, their lack of native language literacy makes it harder, but not undoable, to develop academic literacy in English. They need a targeted program that will develop initial literacy skills and then prepare them for the academic literacy demands of secondary school. They may need extended learning time, with after-school and summer programs to try to catch up with their age-level peers.

Alejandro too faces challenges. His migrant family does not live in the same town for very long. As a child, he switched program types, and that likely hindered his development of literacy skills in either language. Now financial pressures are keeping him from further schooling. His profile is not unlike that of many high school dropouts, and he may need a multifaceted intervention to re-engage with school.

Ignacio, still so young, has a good chance of progressing successfully in school. If his preschool and subsequent elementary school help develop basic literacy skills in both English and Spanish, he will have a strong foundation on which to further develop academic literacy in English. Even if the program mostly uses English as the medium of instruction, Ignacio's parents can promote native language literacy at home by reading books aloud, listening to songs, and conversing with him on a range of topics to widen his conceptual vocabulary base.

In Chapter 2, we describe the sociocultural factors that influence second language acquisition more fully as well as research on second language programs and practices. Here it is important to remember that, in general, English learners with limited formal schooling and below-grade-level literacy skills are most at risk for educational failure. They are entering U.S. schools with weak academic backgrounds at the same time that schools are emphasizing rigorous, standards-based curricula and high-stakes assessments. We want them to have qualified teachers and the best programs possible to enhance their learning opportunities. Our students with native language literacy and on-grade-level abilities cannot be ignored either. They need to be challenged in classes delivered through the new language and supported as they acquire academic literacy in English.

These middle school students use supplementary materials to complete their assignment.

English Learners, Programs, and No Child Left Behind Requirements

Once we learn more about the backgrounds of our English learners, how does what we know about them affect our roles as educators under the No Child Left Behind (NCLB) regulations? The federal definition of a limited English proficient student according to NCLB is the following:

> The learner is between the ages of 3 and 21 and is enrolled or preparing to enroll in an elementary or secondary school. The learner is not academically proficient in English. He or she does not have English as a native language or comes from an environment where English is not dominant or where the environment has a negative impact on proficiency in English. The learner may not have been born in the United States or may be a Native American, Alaskan Native or Pacific Islander. The learner lacks sufficient proficiency in reading, writing, listening, and speaking in English so that the individual is not able to meet the proficient level of achievement on state content assessments and is not able to achieve in the classrooms where the instruction is in English without language supports.

However, it is worth noting that many terms and acronyms are used in districts across the United States to refer to these students and their programs. (See Figure 1.4.)

When schools and districts identify limited English proficient students (referred to as English learners in this book), they are obligated to place students in programs designed according to scientific research. This means the school system must provide English language instruction as well as support in the content areas, either through bilingual instruction or sheltered instruction for these students until they are proficient in

FIGURE 1.4 *Terms and Acronyms for English Learners and Language Development Programs*

EL	English learner
ELL	English language learner
LEP	Limited English proficient
R-LEP	Redesignated limited English proficient (former ELs)
FEP	Fluent English proficient (former ELs)
ESL	English as a second language (may refer to students or program)
ESOL	English speakers of other languages (students)
ESOL	English to speakers of other languages (programs)

English. The language instruction programs must demonstrate their effectiveness by improving the students' English language proficiency (which is assessed annually) and their achievement in core content areas. In requiring this type of accountability, NCLB strives to provide English learners with access to the core content and equal educational opportunities.

The No Child Left Behind Act therefore calls for specialized programs of support so English learners can learn the language and the content of school. NCLB clearly allows for bilingual, dual language, and English as a second language programs as long as they are scientifically based and demonstrate effectiveness. Research, as will be discussed in Chapter 2, suggests that dual language programs, also known as two-way immersion, can be the most effective program type of all, although this model may not be appropriate for all school populations. A careful explication of the different program models for English learners can be found in Genesee, 1999. [See Appendix A for a chart comparing program models.]

NCLB does not put a time limit on how long a student may remain in a language support program. As we reflect on the English learners we described previously, we can see that restricting the time for support could be detrimental to students like Thanh and Alejandro. State departments of education set their own benchmarks for moving students out of the language support program, usually based on certain test scores and teacher recommendations. But often students who make the transition to the regular program are still not completely proficient in academic English and so benefit from being in classes with teachers who can still support their language and literacy development.

According to NCLB, teachers of English language development must be fluent in English and many states require them to be ESL certified. Although the legislation called for highly qualified teachers in every core academic classroom by 2006, neither NCLB nor most states' implementation plans required that elementary classroom and secondary core content teachers have an educational background or training in second language acquisition theory, ESL methodology, or cross-cultural communication, despite the fact that the number of English learners is rising so significantly throughout U.S. schools. Individual states may set that type of requirement, especially in settings where teachers have large numbers of English learners in their math, science, or other content area courses, but to date only Arizona, California, New York, and Florida have done so. Yet it makes sense that a teacher of algebra, for example, with a class full of beginning level English learners should have adequate preparation for addressing the academic and language needs of these students. This preparation may derive from graduate coursework toward an ESL endorsement or a sustained program of professional development.

Sheltered Instruction

One common feature of all effective language support programs for English learners is the goal for eventual success in the English-medium classroom. In order to accomplish this goal, classes that use a sheltered instruction approach are recommended. The sheltered instruction approach is designed for making grade-level, standards-based content material (e.g., math or social studies) more accessible to ELs while at the same time promoting their English language development. The sheltered approach is not simply a set of additional or replacement instructional techniques that teachers implement in their classroom. Effective sheltered instruction draws from and complements high-quality instructional methods advocated for regular classrooms but adds specific strategies for developing English language skills.

Methods that many teachers, in the upper elementary grades and beyond, typically use in class tend not to facilitate literacy instruction or grade-level content learning for beginning learners of English. When teachers rely on oral discourse to present information and organize instruction, it is difficult for many ELs to comprehend. Paper and pencil tasks, like worksheets, are quite challenging if the teachers do not scaffold the learning for students, by making them familiar with the task in advance, for example. Furthermore, students who arrive in the U.S. above grade 3 and are not literate in their native language often find teachers underprepared to teach basic literacy skills to those who missed out on early literacy instruction. By the fourth grade, students are expected to *read to learn*, while they continue to master more sophisticated reading skills. However, many ELs who enter U.S. schools at the upper elementary and secondary grade levels first need to *learn to read*.

So a sheltered approach is a shift in the teaching-learning relationship that requires teachers to engage students in listening, speaking, reading, and writing about the content in meaningful ways with explicit language skill instruction targeted to and a bit beyond the students' level of English proficiency. As students' proficiency in English improves, sheltered instruction teachers should provide less support and organize lessons to help learners become more experienced with academic tasks and routine classroom activities, so it will be easier for them to focus on new content when they make the transition to a regular, English-medium classroom.

In some schools, sheltered instruction is provided to classes composed entirely of English language learners. In others, a mix of native and nonnative English speakers may be present. Bilingual, ESL, or content teachers may be the instructors for these classes (Genesee, 1999). Ideally, all content teachers would be trained in such areas as second language acquisition and ESL methodology, although often that is not the case.

In high-quality sheltered instruction courses, language and content objectives are systematically woven into the curriculum of one particular subject area, such as ninth-grade language arts, U.S. history, fifth-grade mathematics, or life science. Teachers generally present the regular, grade-level subject curriculum to the students through modified instruction in English, although some special curricula may be designed for students with significant gaps in their educational backgrounds or very low literacy skills. Teachers must develop the students' academic language proficiency consistently and regularly as part of the lessons and units that they plan and deliver.

To really make a difference for ELs, sheltered instruction must be part of a broader school-based initiative that takes into account the total schooling they need. Sheltered instruction plays a major role in a variety of educational program designs. It may be part of a content-based ESL program, a late-exit bilingual program, a newcomer program, or a dual language program. Any program where students are learning content through a nonnative language should utilize the sheltered instruction approach.

In some places, these classes may be part of a program known as SEI—structured English immersion, or SDAIE—specially designed academic instruction in English. But SEI and SDAIE are labels; they are not scientifically validated approaches. Empirical research studies have not been conducted on these programs to show they yield a significant positive effect on student achievement. To date, the only scientifically validated approach to sheltered instruction is the SIOP® Model. It offers a replicable framework that can be applied to any classroom where second language learners are learning content through the new language, and it has research evidence of effectiveness regarding student achievement.

The SIOP® Model: Sheltered Instruction for Academic Achievement

Given the diversity among the English learners and their lack of academic success as a group, administrators question what they should do to improve EL achievement and increase English proficiency. In this book, we offer practical and research-based guidance. Research shows that use of the Sheltered Instruction Observation Protocol (SIOP®) Model (Echevarria, Vogt, & Short, 2008), an instructional framework for sheltered instruction, is one component of a systematic approach to effective and appropriate instruction for these learners. Initial research showed that English learners whose teachers were trained in implementing the SIOP® Model performed statistically significantly better on an academic writing assessment than a comparison group of ELs whose teachers had no exposure to the model (Echevarria, Short, & Powers, 2006). More recent research, discussed in Chapter 3, also demonstrates the academic benefits of using the SIOP® Model with English learners.

The SIOP® Model shares many features recommended for high-quality instruction for all students, such as cooperative learning, strategies for reading comprehension, writers' workshop, and differentiated instruction. However, the SIOP® Model adds key features for the academic success of these learners, such as the inclusion of language objectives in every content lesson, the development of background knowledge, the acquisition of content-related vocabulary, and the emphasis on academic literacy practice. The SIOP® Model offers a framework for organizing instruction with required features for each lesson so that teachers can accommodate the distinct second language development needs of the students. The SIOP® Model is composed of thirty features grouped into eight components essential for making content comprehensible for English learners—Lesson Preparation, Building Background, Comprehensible Input, Strategies, Interaction, Practice and Application, Lesson Delivery, and Review and Assessment. A brief explanation of these components is found in the box on page 14. The detailed protocol is found in Appendix B.

Through the SIOP® Model, teachers present standards-based content concepts to ELs using strategies and techniques that make new information comprehensible to the students. While doing so, teachers develop student language skills across the four areas—reading, writing, listening, and speaking. There is not a required script to follow when implementing the SIOP® Model; however, some specific attention to academic literacy development is called for in each SIOP®-designed lesson, particularly in the form of language objectives and subject-specific language use. Moreover, the emphasis that SIOP® lessons place on building vocabulary and background knowledge contribute to the students' literacy development. So a strength of the SIOP® Model is that it allows for

Overview of the SIOP® Model Components and Features

Lesson Preparation: Teachers plan their lessons carefully, including attention to language and content objectives, appropriate content concepts, the use of supplementary materials, adaptation of content, and meaningful activities.

Building Background: Lessons make explicit links to the students' background experiences, knowledge, and past learning, and teach and emphasize key vocabulary.

Comprehensible Input: Lessons incorporate a variety of techniques to make instruction accessible, including speech appropriate to students' English proficiency levels, clear explanations for academic tasks, and the use of visuals, hands-on activities, demonstrations, gestures, and body language.

Strategies: Lessons provide students with instruction in and practice with a variety of learning strategies. Teachers scaffold the delivery of new information and they promote higher-order thinking through a variety of question types and levels.

Interaction: Lessons are designed with frequent opportunities for interaction and discussion among students and with the teacher. Teachers group students to support the content and language objectives, provide sufficient wait time for student responses, and clarify concepts in the student's first language, if possible and as necessary.

Practice and Application: Lessons include hands-on materials and/or manipulatives, and activities for students to apply their content and language knowledge through all language skills (reading, writing, listening, and speaking).

Lesson Delivery: Teachers implement lessons that clearly support content and language objectives with appropriate pacing, while students are engaged 90 to 100 percent of the instructional period.

Review and Assessment: Teachers provide a comprehensive review of key vocabulary and concepts, regularly give specific, academic feedback to students, and conduct assessment of student comprehension and learning throughout the lesson.

natural variation in classroom implementation and pulls together many of the good instructional practices teachers have in their repertoires.

In the following chapters, we will explore the SIOP® Model fully and describe strategies for implementing the model as a professional development initiative at a school or district. We explain the research on second language acquisition and relate the diversity among English learners to the best programs and practices that suit their backgrounds and academic needs.

The Bottom Line

It is important that educational policies and programs reflect the growing body of research on best practices for linguistically diverse students, not political ideologies or language myths. For example, just because our students may sound like native speakers when they converse in the classrooms, it does not mean they are fully proficient in academic English. In addition, the fact that immigrant, non–English-speaking adults obtained jobs with sufficient pay and benefits several generations ago does not mean that today's labor market offers such opportunities to those without strong English skills. The economic reality demands that our high school graduates be literate, educated adults so they can be productive members of society. This means educational practices for ELs must lead toward the goal of high school graduation and proficiency in English.

If schools are to provide a quality education for all children, it is critical that teachers have sufficient preparation to implement empirically sound practices, especially for ELs who consistently underperform in academic settings, and that administrators design and support research-based programs to help the learners. Teachers must accommodate the ELs' varied educational and linguistic backgrounds, take into consideration their second language acquisition needs, and employ research-based instruction such as the SIOP® Model so that they deliver lessons that are meaningful and appropriate for these students.

Key Points Summary

- More and more students learning English as a new language are enrolled in our schools. In general, their academic achievement has been below the average performance level of native English speakers.
- Not all English learners are alike. Individual characteristics such as literacy in the first language and educational background affect how quickly ELs will acquire academic English and be successful in school.
- Appropriate program models and instructional practices are needed for English learners so they develop academic literacy in English. This includes targeted instruction for content and language development.
- To date, the SIOP® Model is the only approach to teaching language and content to English learners that has been validated by empirical research that measured student achievement outcomes.

Reflect and Apply

1. Perform a needs analysis on your academic program that serves English learners. Consider one school with a large number of ELs. How many teachers have had sufficient training to work with them? What areas of staff development would benefit them? How many courses have sheltered curricula? On average, how many years do ELs at that school spend in a language support program? When they exit, are they adequately prepared for the work of a mainstream classroom? If not, what would improve their performance?

2. Look at your school, district, and state test scores over the past five years. How have the English learners been doing over that time? Can you attribute changes in their performance to any specific initiatives? In which areas are improvements still needed?

chapter 2

Learning a Second Language

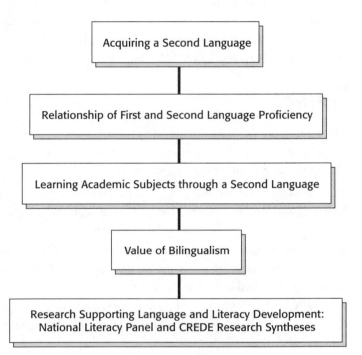

Acquiring a Second Language

Relationship of First and Second Language Proficiency

Learning Academic Subjects through a Second Language

Value of Bilingualism

Research Supporting Language and Literacy Development:
National Literacy Panel and CREDE Research Syntheses

Objectives

After reading, discussing, and reflecting on this chapter, you will be able to meet the following content and language objectives.

Content Objective:

Administrators will identify ways that teachers in their schools provide opportunities for students to practice using academic English in meaningful ways.

Language Objective:

Administrators will describe several factors that affect second language acquisition.

Marisela sits in class trying her hardest to understand what the teacher is talking about. She told her mother just this morning that she is determined to do well in school for herself and for her family. When she arrived last year it was difficult to keep up but this year was going to be different. Marisela sometimes feels like her whole body is affected as she struggles to reach beyond what she knows and apply that to a new language, culture, way of thinking and acting. She wants to do well on her homework but she is so physically tired at the end of a day—a day spent in intense concentration—that she often has to take a nap. So much of what the teacher says is difficult to understand, and his writing on the board is small and hard to read. Marisela wishes he would use the overhead projector like her teacher last year did to give her clues about what is expected. Sometimes that teacher would model an activity or show a sample of the work they had to do. This year, the other students seem to understand what to do so Marisela is often embarrassed to ask for clarification. She knows she's smart because she helps her mother pay the bills at home and has responsibilities that she takes care of proudly, but at school she feels timid and unsure. So every day she begins by telling herself that she will learn more English and will complete the day's assignments the best she can.

Acquiring a Second Language

Learning a second language is a long and complicated process. Sending and receiving messages (which is what language actually is) in a second language requires a great deal of effort; a total physical, emotional, and intellectual response (Brown, 2000). In addition to learning to listen, speak, read, and write in English, there are new ways of using the language, called pragmatics, which must be learned. For example, there are variations in cultures with respect to politeness, humor, subtle communication acts, degrees of formality, and the like. Overall, students who are acquiring fluency in English are participating in a complex, difficult process that takes many years to achieve. These students, as mentioned in Chapter 1, vary in their language and learning abilities, and many struggle to be successful in our schools.

As administrators, it is important to understand the process of second language learning because of its relevance to all learning. One cannot be expected to achieve academically or perform well on standardized assessments if his or her level of English proficiency is well below what is needed to even understand the instructions of an assignment or test. During an interview on implementing the SIOP® Model (Echevarria, Short, & Vogt, 2008), one district administrator who had served as director of services for ELs in a number of large districts made this poignant comment:

> Administrators need to understand second language acquisition—and really understand what academic language is—before they can put it on "the front burner" with their staff. Once they get it, they will see how important it is for English learners' achievement. Having an understanding of second language acquisition isn't only for ESL specialists or teachers of ELs. Administrators must learn what English learners need to be successful in school.

Language Skills

Second language learning involves listening, speaking, reading, and writing in the target language. This includes skills in

- **Speaking and listening, namely oral language development.** Language is involved in most everything we do from thinking ("Should I stop for gas?") to communicating with others ("I'd like to order lunch now") to solving problems ("To find the average cost, I'll add these numbers then divide"). In fact, language is the primary way that intellectual development is facilitated. Opportunities to practice using oral language are critical because oral language provides the foundation for language development. Since language development is an active, not passive, process, students acquiring a second language benefit from structured opportunities to use language in meaningful ways in small groups at their level of proficiency. Both expressive (speaking) and receptive (listening with understanding) skills are enhanced through oral interaction with others. English learners enter school with at least a five-year gap in English oral skills. Native English speakers have had five years of practice with oral English before entering kindergarten, giving them an advantage over their EL counterparts. For older ELs, the gap is even wider. This is why it is all the more important for ELs to have consistent opportunities to develop oral language skills in English.

● **Reading.** The National Reading Panel (National Institute of Child Health and Human Development, 2000) defined the components of reading as phonics, phonemic awareness, fluency, vocabulary, and reading comprehension. Research suggests that high-quality instruction in these five components generally works for English learners as well, with some considerations or accommodations such as more focus on oral language development and visual representations of words to enhance comprehension. These findings are further detailed in the Report of the National Literacy Panel on Language-Minority Children & Youth (August & Shanahan, 2006).

While English learners are able to attain well-taught word-level skills equal to their English-speaking peers such as decoding, word recognition, and spelling, the same is not typically the case with text-level skills such as reading comprehension and writing. The reason for the disparity between word-level and text-level skills among English learners is oral English proficiency. Well-developed oral proficiency in English, that is English vocabulary knowledge, listening comprehension and syntactic skills, is associated with English reading and writing proficiency. So it is not enough to teach English learners the components of reading alone. Teachers must incorporate extensive oral language development opportunities into literacy instruction. Further, English learners benefit from having word meanings clarified with picture cues; having extra practice reading words, sentences, and stories; and consolidating text knowledge through summarization. Since reading is the foundation for learning in school, it is critical that teachers use research-based practices to provide English learners with high-quality instruction that will lead to development of strong reading skills.

● **Writing.** The statistics about English learners cited in Chapter 1 make it clear that it takes many years to develop grade-level English skills, and writing is an area that is affected significantly by limited English proficiency. While oral skills can be developed as students engage in meaningful activities, skills in writing must be explicitly taught. The writing process, which involves planning, drafting, editing, and revising written work, allows students to express their ideas at their level of proficiency with teacher (or peer) guidance and explicit corrective feedback. However, for English learners, it is critical that a lot of meaningful discussion takes place prior to asking students to write because such dialogue leads to writing and provides students with the English words they will use. Writing is also facilitated by such techniques as teacher modeling, posting of writing samples, providing sentence frames, and even having students copy words or text until they gain more independent proficiency (Graham & Perin, 2007). This kind of constant exposure to words and sentence patterning allows ELs to become familiar with the conventions of how words and sentences are put together in the language (Garcia & Beltran, 2003).

The interdependence of listening, speaking, reading, and writing is clear, and these four language processes are best approached as a totality, not as separate entities. English learners should be encouraged to write in English early, especially if they have skills in their native language, and should be provided frequent opportunities to express their ideas in writing. Errors in writing are to be expected and should be viewed as part of the natural process of acquisition (Crawford, 2003). Teachers who are sensitive to the second language acquisition process understand that English learners will make errors in speaking and accept it as part of the development of English skills. The same applies to writing. As mentioned above, corrective feedback is important but overcorrection—especially of expected, developmental types of errors such as *eskool* for *school*—can be discouraging for students learning to write in English and should be avoided.

Vocabulary Development

We know from research and common sense how valuable a robust knowledge of vocabulary is. A rich and varied vocabulary is an important part of language development and is essential to academic success. English learners require more repetition and repeated exposures to vocabulary words than do native speakers of English, so oral language practice using new words is essential.

For a student to comprehend a text that he or she reads independently, researchers found that the student needs to know 90 to 95 percent of the words (Nagy & Scott, 2000). This is a difficult proposition for beginning and intermediate-level English learners. Among native English speakers, it has been shown that eighth graders, on average, have a reading vocabulary of 25,000 word families; twelfth graders, a reading vocabulary of 50,000 word families (Graves, 2006). A word family is a basic word and all of its other forms and meanings. So the word family for *go* includes go, went, gone, going, going out, go on, go over, gone by, and so forth.

In general, students with better vocabularies are more successful on tests and other measures of achievement. We know that teaching vocabulary can improve reading comprehension for native English speakers (Beck, Perfetti, & McKeown, 1982) and for English language learners (Carlo et al., 2004). However, there is a lot more vocabulary to learn than teachers can teach our English learners, particularly those who are at the beginning level in secondary school. Therefore, we need to instruct students in word learning and word awareness strategies and in cognate recognition and use. We have to help them develop knowledge of words and how they work, so the students understand content area topics and assignments and develop strong reading comprehension and test-taking skills (Graves, 2006).

Conversational and Academic Language

One perplexing issue in schools is the number of students who seem to have learned English—or at least are able to communicate sufficiently—but are underperforming academically. For many of these students, a reason for this discrepancy may be that they have developed conversational ability but lack the academic language necessary for school success. The conversational/academic distinction recognizes that students acquire basic interpersonal communicative skills, known as BICS or conversational language, relatively quickly. However, the academic language necessary for school tasks such as reading, writing, mathematics, and other content subjects is referred to as cognitive academic language proficiency (CALP), a more complex type of language knowledge that takes longer to acquire (Cummins, 2000).

Academic language is best learned through wide reading experiences with a variety of genres and direct teaching of academic vocabulary that facilitates understanding of words, concepts, and information. Standards-based instruction is based on hefty amounts of academic language, so achievement is predicated upon students' acquisition of this important type of language.

Relationship of First and Second Language Proficiency

FIGURE 2.1 *Factors That Influence Second Language Acquisition*

| Motivation |
| Access to the language |
| Age |
| Personality |
| First language develop- |
| ment |
| Quality of instruction |
| Cognitive ability |

Second language acquisition is a very complex process, and its success or failure cannot be explained by a single factor or theory (Long, 2007). Many factors influence students' acquisition of English (Echevarria & Graves, 2007) such as those in Figure 2.1 and discussed below.

Motivation

While there is great variation in motivational levels from learner to learner, the importance of high motivation for second language acquisition and learning is clear, especially considering how long and hard students must work to reach grade-level proficiency. In particular, motivation has been found to influence reading comprehension for English learners (Lesaux, Koda, Siegel, & Shanahan, 2006), which is an important determinant of academic success.

What are motives for learning a second language and learning in a second language? Baker (1992) discusses two types of motivation: integrative and instrumental. When students are motivated to identify with or join another language—that is, integrate into the group—the process is termed *integrative motivation*. For example, children may be highly motivated to learn English so they can join in playground activities with their classmates, participate in classroom assignments with peers, or interact socially at high school events. This type of motivation increases the likelihood of becoming proficient in the second language because it involves developing personal relationships that are potentially long lasting.

In contrast, *instrumental motivation* describes how individuals learn another language for practical reasons such as getting a job, enhancing career possibilities, or passing a high-stakes exam. This type of motivation may not be as effective in leading to mastery of the second language since it tends to involve short-term goals. Once a goal is achieved—the exam is passed, the job is obtained—motivation for learning English may diminish, unless another goal replaces it (e.g., getting a promotion).

In addition to motives that the student brings, the instructional environment of the school or classroom has a significant impact on students' motivational levels. Features that create conditions for optimal learning include the following (Zadina, 2004):

- High expectations
- Respect for students and teachers, their cultures, home lives, and languages
- Safe and welcoming school environment
- Students' ownership and sense of control over learning
- Positive social bonding
- Encouragement—"You can do this!", "Your success matters to me!"

- Self-discipline and capacity to delay gratification
- Sense of connectedness
- Playfulness, joy

When these conditions are present, students may be more motivated to participate in instructional tasks and actively engage in learning.

Age

Debate continues regarding the optimal age for beginning second language acquisition. However, there is little controversy about some basic facts of age differences in second language learning. A number of studies have shown that while young children are more efficient at aspects of language acquisition related to settings for conversation such as the home and playground where they interact naturally with native speakers, they make slower progress in the initial stages of learning the grammar of a new language. If they start early enough, time and exposure can eventually lead to achieving high levels of proficiency, even native-like levels. Older children and adults tend to learn faster in the early stages, perhaps because of their advanced cognitive abilities and larger repertoire of learning strategies, but few achieve near native-like proficiency. They frequently have a detectable accent, have smaller vocabularies and tend to make some grammatical errors, even after many years of study or use (Fillmore & Snow, 2002; Krashen, 1982; Long, 2007). Researchers do not as yet agree on exactly how early one must begin learning a second language to reach maximum results.

Access to the Language

Opportunities for learning English are promoted by successful communicative exchanges with native English speakers. The classroom provides an ideal setting for such exchanges when teachers use heterogeneous groupings (native speakers with nonnative speakers) and create a learning environment that encourages student-to-student interaction. In fact for English learners, especially recent immigrants, schools may be the primary source of contact with the majority culture, thus playing a role in acculturation (Phinney, Romero, Nava, & Huang, 2001) in addition to providing language learning opportunities.

In order to participate fully in class, English learners need to develop sufficient vocabulary skills in English to access grade-level content since vocabulary impacts reading, writing, speaking, and listening. One major determinant of poor reading comprehension for English learners and for lagging readers is limited vocabulary (Nagy, 1997; National Reading Panel, 2000). Since reading comprehension and vocabulary knowledge are strongly correlated (Biemiller, 2001; Stahl, 1999), weak vocabularies prevent many English learners from comprehending texts, resulting in little or no understanding of literature, scientific processes, math instructions and word problems, historical descriptions—essentially the content material taught throughout the school day.

Personality

Extroverts may enjoy initial success with language learning because they tend to prefer the social aspects of relationships, such as talking, playing, and working with others. Thus, these students have increased opportunities for interaction with English speakers. However, research to date does not show long-term language learning differences based on introversion and extroversion.

Risk-taking is a personality characteristic that does affect language learning. A willingness to experiment with English vocabulary and forms of the language, as well as drawing generalizations from what has been learned, improves proficiency. Those who take risks with using the new language and then receive positive reinforcement for their attempts are more likely to use the language again. Thus, using the language helps promote language acquisition.

First Language Development

Learning a first language is a complex task requiring a minimum of twelve years, and aspects of development such as vocabulary expansion extend language learning throughout a lifetime. Although a tremendous amount of language is acquired from birth to age five, children from ages six to twelve continue to develop more complex forms of semantics, phonology, morphology, and syntax as well as more elaborate speech acts. See Figure 2.2.

One's level of first language development significantly influences second language development. Students who have had solid schooling in their native language are more efficient at acquiring a new language. Further, those who have home literacy experiences and literacy opportunities generally achieve superior literacy outcomes (Goldenberg, Rueda, & August, 2006). Individuals who achieve full cognitive development in both languages will gain cognitive benefits, but when development of the first language is discontinued, there may actually be negative consequences (Collier, 1987). Native-language oral proficiency and literacy can facilitate the development of literacy in English (August & Shanahan, 2006).

FIGURE 2.2   *Forms of Language*

Semantics—meaning or interpretation of a word or sentence. For example, *She is always there and is my most defensible friend* has an error in semantics. The word *defensible* should have been *dependable* to carry the correct meaning.
Phonology—speech sounds or the sound system of a language. For example, pronouncing *apple* with a long *a* would be a phonological error.
Morphology—structure and form of words and word parts in language. For example, *Yesterday the three men walk across the street* is incorrect. The correct form of the verb would be *walked* to indicate past tense.
Syntax—word order or grammatical arrangement of words in a sentence. For example, *The man went to the drugstore* is correct but *Went the man to the store drug* is incorrect.

Quality of Instruction

What happens in the classroom is vitally important for English learners. The teacher's daily routines, level of lesson preparation, expectations for students, use of instructional strategies, knowledge of the subject matter, and techniques for modifying instruction for

English learners all have an impact on learning outcomes, including language acquisition. The challenge for teachers of students with diverse abilities is to create classroom conditions in which learners can and will learn by adjusting texts, tasks, and instructional settings to match the learners' needs (Lipson & Wixson, 2007; Vogt & Shearer, 2007). Saunders & Goldenberg (2001) found that there are four elements essential to academic success for English learners. Teachers should

- build students' background knowledge;
- draw on students' personal experiences;
- promote extended discourse through writing and discussion; and
- assist students in rereading pivotal portions of a text.

It has been suggested that many learning problems experienced by ELs are pedagogically induced, or the result of instructional practices unsuited to the learner, resulting in inappropriate placement in special education (Cummins, 1984). If instruction is not made comprehensible and accessible for students, the opportunity to learn both English and content material decreases. Learning outcomes for English learners are enhanced in classrooms where features of the SIOP® Model are put into practice on a regular basis, building English skills while at the same time developing content knowledge.

Student achievement is also facilitated by a knowledgeable and skillful teacher. Good teachers make the difference, and prepared teachers are effective teachers. For English learners, skillful teachers provide opportunities for students to learn language by using it in meaningful ways including group or cooperative learning experiences. They build on students' prior knowledge and link the content to what students already know or have experienced; and they use a variety of techniques to make the language understandable, such as graphic organizers, media (especially video clips), and visual displays of information (Tellez & Waxman, 2006).

Finally, research has found that schools need structured, sustained, intensive professional development to yield high-quality instruction. The process should include peer teacher observations and being part of a network where teachers share together, grow together, and learn to respect each other's work (Echevarria, Short, & Vogt, 2008; Wong, 2003).

Cognitive Ability

Many of the underlying cognitive processes that are important for second language acquisition are related to general cognitive abilities, such as verbal memory, phonological awareness, and categorization. These abilities affect the language learning process (Genesee, Geva, Dressler, & Kamil, 2006), although wide variation among learners is expected. Individuals with lower cognitive ability are capable of acquiring a second language, but proficiency levels would not likely exceed those in the first language.

Extreme caution should be used in ascribing low ability labels to English learners. Many of the tasks that require cognitive ability also tap background knowledge and experience. So, for many English learners, they may not have had the requisite background experiences or knowledge to make sense of an academic task, but this in no way indicates low cognitive ability.

It is important for administrators to understand that the factors discussed in this section account for some of the diversity in English learners described in Chapter 1.

Moreover, these factors impact daily instruction in the classroom. English learners are not a homogeneous category of students. They have different levels of access to standard English, they began learning English at different ages, and they differ in how well developed literacy is in their first language. Some students are more motivated than others to learn English, and students vary in innate ability. These factors should be considered as instruction is tailored to students' academic and linguistic needs.

Learning Academic Subjects through a Second Language

Relatively few administrators have had the experience of learning new, challenging material in a language other than English. Imagine if an important legal document from the state department of education arrived addressed to you but when you opened the contents, you found it was written in German or Cantonese. Think of the difficulty in trying to decipher what the document said, especially in a language you presumably don't understand. Sometimes such documents are difficult to decipher in English!

English learners have experiences similar to this every day. They can understand information and concepts when other clues are present, such as visuals or demonstrations, but a page filled with words written in English may be difficult to understand, even with intermediate proficiency in the language.

Communicative tasks (listening, speaking, reading, and writing) have varying levels of contextual support and cognitive demand difficulty (Cummins, 2000). This range of communicative demands is conceptualized in Figure 2.3 and is based on Cummins's framework.

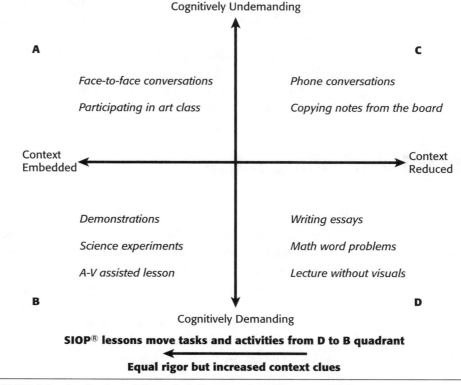

FIGURE 2.3 *Application of Cummins's Framework to Classroom Settings*

The communicative tasks and activities in the upper quadrants (A and C) represent those that require less active cognitive involvement, depending on the level of context provided, while the communicative tasks and activities in the lower quadrants (B and D) represent those that require more active cognitive involvement. The horizontal continuum represents support ranging from contextually embedded communication, where meaning can be derived from a variety of clues (such as gestures, visual cues, and feedback), to context-reduced communication that relies primarily on spoken words or written texts that give few if any contextual clues. For example, a page of text without pictures or other visual clues doesn't have meaning if the reader does not understand the language.

The vertical continuum relates to the cognitive demands of the task. For example, an easy (cognitively undemanding) task can be performed with little or no conscious thought, such as reciting one's name and phone number. These activities and tasks have become automatized. Moving to the other end of the vertical continuum, a task like attempting to understand a lecture on an unfamiliar scientific topic is cognitively demanding.

How might Cummins's framework for language apply to instructional situations in the classroom? Tasks and activities in the A quadrant should be relatively easy for English learners, since they require little active cognitive involvement and are supported by contextual clues. However, the most prevalent types of instructional tasks and activities are found in quadrant D; they are also the most difficult. These tasks and activities offer few contextual clues and may include reading a text (without visual clues or other types of text support), understanding and applying scientific concepts, doing math word problems, writing essays, listening to lectures to gain information, and taking tests.

With the SIOP® Model, tasks and activities that would be quite difficult for English learners (found in the D quadrant; difficult tasks with few clues) are made more understandable by creating a context for learners (moved into the B quadrant; difficult tasks with ample clues). Instructional tasks and activities in the B quadrant are as rigorous as those in the D quadrant but provide the contextual clues that assist English learners in being successful academically. Thus, challenging, difficult material is presented in ways that make it understandable, including modeling tasks and procedures, using visuals for context, hands-on activities, history projects, and science labs. These types of activities and tasks do not "water down" the curriculum but instead make grade-level concepts and information understandable and accessible.

The Value of Bilingualism

There are obvious benefits to being able to read, write, speak, and understand more than one language. These benefits extend beyond school to social settings, employment opportunities, broad cultural and learning experiences, and more. Bilingualism is "not just a societal resource, it is also an individual resource that potentially can enhance aspects of bilingual children's academic, cognitive and linguistic functioning" (Cummins, 2000, p. 175).

Research findings confirm that teaching academic skills such as reading in the first language is more effective for second language achievement than simply immersing students in English instruction (August & Shanahan, 2006). So time spent in high-quality native language literacy instruction isn't time "lost" for English proficiency development.

Gunston Middle School values and celebrates multilingualism and multiculturalism.

In fact, it can speed up proficiency in the long run. The *linguistic interdependence hypothesis* (Cummins, 2000) holds that academic language skills learned in the native language will transfer to the new language (English) and that skills are interdependent across languages. For example, once a child has learned to read in her native language, she can then learn to read in other similar languages (i.e., those with similar alphabets) without relearning skills such as the concept of sound-symbol relationships. Other concepts such as subtracting with regrouping in math or recognizing the functions of cell parts will transfer to the second language as well. The process of transfer, however, is neither automatic nor inevitable (Gersten, Brengelman, & Jimenez, 1994). It is a process that requires guidance by a skilled teacher with explicit links made to past learning. For students to draw on previously learned concepts, skills, or information, they frequently need prompting, reminders, and explicit teaching.

Research on Language and Literacy Development: The National Literacy Panel and CREDE Research Syntheses

The challenge of educating growing numbers of English learners has become a priority for many administrators. But what are effective, research-based practices for meeting this challenge? Researchers have recently addressed that question by summarizing and synthesizing empirical studies of English learners. Findings of the National Literacy Panel on Language-Minority Children and Youth (August & Shanahan, 2006) and the research synthesis from the Center for Research on Education, Diversity & Excellence (Genesee, Saunders, Lindholm-Leary, & Christian, 2006) provide guidance to schools regarding effective instructional practices that lead to achievement gains for English learners. In this section, we summarize the research findings related to second language learning.

- In the area of word-level components of literacy, such as decoding or spelling, ELs can reach levels equal to their monolingual peers, with appropriate instruction.

- Oral language skills are an important aspect of literacy development.
- English learners benefit from instruction in the components of reading that are recommended by the National Reading Panel (i.e., phonics, phonemic awareness, vocabulary, fluency, and text comprehension).
- Instruction in these components of reading is necessary but not sufficient for English learners to become proficient readers and writers in English. Oral proficiency in English is important as well.
- Language limitations affect reading progress as students move through the grade levels. Therefore, vocabulary development is critical for English learners to attain grade-level literacy.
- Three findings relate the role of the home language to literacy development:
  - Language minority parents are willing and in many cases able to help their children achieve academically. Schools tend to underestimate and underutilize parents' potential contributions.
  - More home literacy experiences and opportunities are associated with superior literacy outcomes, although the findings are inconsistent. However, parent education level does influence children's literacy outcomes.
  - The relationship between home language use and literacy achievement in English is unclear. Studies had somewhat conflicting results regarding the impact of native language use on the development of literacy in English.

In their role as instructional leaders, administrators can utilize the research on second language acquisition and literacy presented in this chapter by providing teachers with current information about best practices for English learners. Further, classroom observations and the quality of feedback provided to teachers of English learners will be more effective when administrators are better equipped to understand the instructional needs of these students.

Key Points Summary

- English learners are working very hard to process information in a new language. This cognitive load can be physically, emotionally, and mentally draining.
- Learning a second language is a long and complicated process. In addition to learning to listen, speak, read, and write in English, new ways of using the language must also be learned.
- There is a critical difference between conversational and academic language proficiency. Using English socially does not equate with being able to perform academic tasks successfully.
- Learning is facilitated with more context clues. Teachers of English learners should frequently use modeling, visuals, and repetition as well as provide opportunities for students to practice using academic English in meaningful ways.
- Support and clarification in students' native language contributes to learning academic content in English.

- Development of vocabulary is an essential component of effective instruction for English learners and accounts for academic achievement.
- English learners need many opportunities to use authentic language throughout the school day to develop oral English skills.

Reflect and Apply

1. Think about a lesson you have recently observed. How much time did the teacher spend on vocabulary development with English learners? Were there sufficient opportunities to practice and develop oral language skills? How could the teacher have facilitated more learning for the English learners in the class?

2. Some students seem to learn English quickly and achieve academically while others continue to struggle after months, perhaps years. What are several factors that may have an impact on the rate of English acquisition?

3. The National Literacy Panel reported findings about parents of English learners. In your own school or district, what are some barriers to parental involvement? How can you involve parents to a greater extent?

Understanding the SIOP® Model

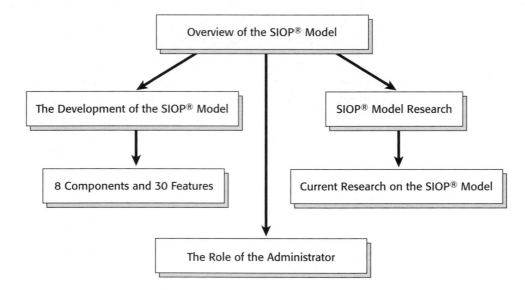

I was introduced to the SIOP® Model while completing my 15 hours in Structured English Immersion, which is needed for certification according to Arizona requirements (for all educators). I thought it was going to be just another inservice, but I was pleasantly surprised. It just made sense. It was a systematic way to teaching that was teacher friendly. This model is a benefit to students in that it breaks all the components into manageable sections that could be learned, implemented, and assessed over time. It was not an immediate intervention but a tool for continuous learning. Also, with the focus on learning and teaching, strategies to systematically integrate reading, writing, listening, and speaking increase student engagement while simultaneously increasing student language development and academic achievement. Using the SIOP® Model to support teachers will benefit student learning because it will transfer teacher lecturing into the hands of student learning, literally.

David McNeil, Principal, Washington Middle School

In this chapter we provide an overview of the SIOP® Model's eight components and thirty features, review the original and current research on the model, and offer guidance for observing SIOP® lessons.

Overview of the SIOP® Model

Schools and districts that serve English learners have been informed that they should utilize programs that are "scientifically based," namely those with research evidence of student success. However, few interventions designed specifically for English learners have collected, analyzed, and published achievement data on ELs to date. That is why the SIOP® Model offers such promise. In the national research study for the Center for Research on Education, Diversity & Excellence (CREDE), students who had content teachers trained in this specific approach to sheltered instruction—the SIOP® Model—performed significantly better on a standardized state academic writing assessment than a comparison group of similar students in classes with teachers not trained in the model. In subsequent studies, the SIOP® Model has had a positive impact on English learner achievement as well.

The Development of the SIOP® Model

The CREDE-sponsored research study "The Effects of Sheltered Instruction on the Achievement of Limited English Proficient Students" began in 1996 with the following goals:

1. Design an explicit model of sheltered instruction that teachers could use to improve the academic success of English language learners,

2. Train teachers in that model, and

3. Measure the effects of the new model on student achievement.

The research plan was to design a model that would be applicable for all subject areas and would offer a framework for instruction that incorporates the best instructional practice for teaching both language and content. This intervention would help English learners acquire content knowledge while they develop and improve academic English language skills. By the mid-1990s when we began the research, teachers had a wide variety of techniques and methods in their pedagogical repertoires for making content comprehensible, but no set structure for organizing sheltered lessons consistently with the dual goals of content learning and English language development. We did not know then which combination of techniques would be most beneficial for English learners. We sought to find the answer.

The seven-year research project involved the active collaboration of practicing middle school teachers in refining the model for sheltered instruction and field-testing it in their classrooms. First, we developed a research observation instrument, the Sheltered Instruction Observation Protocol (SIOP®), so that we could determine how well teachers were including features of effective sheltered instruction in their lessons. The SIOP® features incorporated in the observation tool were determined by the literature on best practices, such as scaffolding, cooperative learning, literacy techniques, and use of meaningful curricula and materials. We created a scale for each feature (4 to 0) so we could measure the level of implementation in any given lesson (4 being closest to recommended practice, 0 being no evidence of the use of the practice).

Early on in the project, we requested that another researcher lead a study to establish the validity and reliability of the Sheltered Instruction Observation Protocol instrument.

FIGURE 3.1 *SIOP® Terminology*

> **SIOP® Model**—lesson planning and delivery system for the research-based approach to sheltered instruction, composed of eight components and thirty features of effective instruction for English learners.
>
> **SIOP® protocol**—instrument used to observe and rate sheltered instruction lessons on the thirty features using a numeric scale; this tool has been validated and found to be reliable through a research process.

Teacher education faculty who were not part of the CREDE research but who had expertise in sheltered instruction served as raters. A statistical analysis revealed an inter-rater agreement of .99. Additional analyses indicated that the SIOP® instrument is a highly reliable and valid measure of sheltered instruction (Guarino, Echevarria, Short, Schick, Forbes, & Rueda, 2001).

Based on feedback from the collaborating teacher-researcher teams in several districts on the East and West Coasts, the observation instrument evolved into a lesson planning tool, known as the SIOP® Model (Echevarria, Vogt, & Short, 2000, 2004, 2008; Short & Echevarria, 1999; 2004/2005). "If you are going to observe us using the SIOP®," one of the project teachers had said, "shouldn't we use it to plan our lessons?" Indeed. So we organized the SIOP® into a lesson planning system, and the acronym SIOP® began being used by teachers as its own word. We now refer to the SIOP® Model as the lesson planning and delivery approach to instruction and the SIOP® protocol as the observation rating tool. (See Figure 3.1.)

We also developed and field-tested a professional development program for the SIOP® Model. This program incorporates an effective teacher development approach as recommended by Darling-Hammond (1998) and Garet, Porter, Desimone, Birman, & Yoon (2001). Through sustained interaction among SIOP®-trained staff developers and teachers (for at least one year in most cases), we found that teachers could modify their pedagogy to promote both language and content learning among the English learners. This professional development program is being used in school districts throughout the United States and in several sites abroad. Details about SIOP® implementation in some of these districts and others can be found in *Implementing the SIOP® Model through Effective Professional Development and Coaching* (Echevarria, Short, & Vogt, 2008).

The SIOP® Model: Eight Components and Thirty Features

As previewed in Chapter 1, the SIOP® Model is composed of thirty features grouped into eight components essential for making content comprehensible for English learners: Lesson Preparation, Building Background, Comprehensible Input, Strategies, Interaction, Practice and Application, Lesson Delivery, and Review and Assessment. A full explanation of each component and feature, including the theoretical and research background as well as practical applications, can be found in *Making Content Comprehensible for English Learners: The SIOP® Model* (Echevarria, Vogt, & Short, 2008). Appendix B in this book includes the comprehensive and abbreviated forms of the Sheltered Instruction Observation Protocol. By considering the indicators of the rating scale, you can begin to understand how closely a lesson might meet the SIOP® Model.

The following discussion provides an overview of the model as teachers would use it for their lessons.

Lesson Preparation. Teachers plan SIOP® lessons with language and content objectives linked to state curriculum standards that are posted and discussed daily with students. In this way, students know what they are expected to learn and can take an active part in assessing their own progress. Through these lessons, students gain important experience with key grade-level content and skills as they progress toward proficiency in the second language. Teachers include supplementary materials, such as trade books, models, and audiovisual and computer-based resources, and adapt the content or tasks to improve comprehensibility. Planned activities must be meaningful and need to prepare ELs for content area classes by giving them practice with the academic language, tasks, and topics they will encounter in those classes.

Building Background. Effective SIOP® lessons connect new concepts with the students' personal experiences and past learning. The SIOP® Model underscores the importance of building a broad vocabulary base for students to be effective readers, writers, speakers, and listeners. In the SIOP® Model, teachers directly teach key vocabulary and word structures, word families, and word relationships. Lesson activities should provide opportunities for students to use this vocabulary orally and in writing and through different learning modes, because students need twelve or more practice opportunities with new words in order to learn to use them on their own (Graves, 2006).

Comprehensible Input. Accomplished SIOP® teachers use sheltered and ESL techniques to make content comprehensible, including

- demonstrations and modeling;
- gestures, pantomime, and role-play;
- visual aids such as illustrations, real objects, graphs and charts, video and other media;
- graphic organizers;
- restating, repeating, and reducing the speed of the teacher's presentation;
- previewing important information; and
- hands-on, experiential activities.

SIOP® teachers adjust their speech to the students' proficiency levels and explain academic tasks clearly, both orally and in writing, providing models and examples of good work so students know the steps they should take and can envision the desired result.

Strategies. To equip students for learning outside of the language development classroom, the SIOP® Model calls for explicit instruction and practice in learning strategies. Good reading comprehension strategies, for example, need to be modeled and practiced, with authentic text. SIOP® teachers must scaffold instruction so students can become more independent learners, by initiating instruction at the students' current performance level and providing support to move them to a higher level of understanding and accomplishment. Teachers have to ask critical-thinking questions as well so that students apply their language skills while developing a deeper understanding of the subject topics.

Interaction. Students learn through interaction with one another and with their teachers. They need extensive oral language practice to deepen content and vocabulary knowledge. Teachers provide models of appropriate speech, word choice, intonation, and fluency, but student-student interaction is also important and needs to occur regularly so ELs can practice academic language functions, such as clarifying information, negotiating meaning, and evaluating opinions. The interaction features remind teachers to encourage elaborated speech, to group students appropriately for language and content development, and to provide sufficient wait time for students to process questions and answers in their new language. Furthermore, teachers should allow students to clarify information using their native language when necessary to assist them with comprehension.

Practice and Application. Practice and application of new material is critical for all learners. Our SIOP® Model research found that lessons with hands-on, visual, and other kinesthetic tasks benefit English learners because students practice the language and content knowledge through multiple modalities. Effective SIOP® lessons, therefore, include a variety of activities that encourage students to not only practice and apply the content they are learning, but also practice and apply their language skills. It is important for lessons to build and reinforce reading, writing, listening, and speaking skills together.

Lesson Delivery. Successful delivery of a SIOP® lesson means that the content and language objectives were met, the pacing was appropriate, and the students had a high level of engagement. The art of teaching and classroom management skills play a role in effective lesson delivery. Having routines, making sure students know the lesson objectives so they can stay on track, and designing meaningful activities that appeal to students are helpful strategies. Time should not be wasted, yet a lesson should not move so swiftly that the students don't understand the key information.

Review and Assessment. Each SIOP® lesson should wrap up with dedicated time for review and assessment. English learners need to revisit key vocabulary and concepts, and teachers need to use frequent comprehension checks and other informal assessments to measure how well students retain the information. Accomplished SIOP® teachers also offer multiple pathways for students to demonstrate their understanding of the content. Sometimes students are assessed in writing, sometimes orally. Assessments should look at the range of language and content development, including measures of vocabulary, grammar, comprehension skills, and content concepts.

The Role of the ESL Teacher

Language is the key to learning in schools; we primarily learn through language and use language to demonstrate our knowledge. As Lemke (1988, p. 81) pointed out,

> . . .educators have begun to realize that the mastery of academic subjects is the mastery of their specialized patterns of language use, and that language is the dominant medium through which these subjects are taught and students' mastery of them tested.

Lemke's words are particularly true for students learning English as a new language while they are learning academic content. That is why although we had content area teachers of ELs initially in mind when we designed the SIOP® Model, we realized early on that language teachers are essential partners for the English learners' academic success. The content teachers need to pay attention to how language is used in their discipline and make it explicit to the ELs; the language teachers need to build vocabulary and background knowledge for the content courses their students take while they teach academic English.

We strongly encourage ESL teachers to incorporate the SIOP® features through content-based ESL. These ESL lessons, like the sheltered content ones, should have both language and content objectives and utilize all the other features of the SIOP® Model too. ESL teachers would draw objectives from the ESL state standards but also design lessons that support the content knowledge students need in their other courses at school. ESL teachers, for example, might plan thematic units on topics such as the ecology of the rain forest or the civil rights movement. Content objectives could be drawn from life sciences, history, and mathematics. Lessons would also provide ELs with practice in the academic skills and tasks common to mainstream classes. Throughout the course syllabus, a range of different content topics would be covered with a focus on both form and function of academic language as used within the content themes.

Content-based ESL and sheltered content instruction represent the two sides of a coin for integrated language and content teaching and learning. One focuses more on proficiency in the new language; the other, comprehension of grade-level subject curricula. Together, these courses are a promising combination for EL success when implemented throughout a school.

SIOP® Model Research

After finalizing the SIOP® Model as a lesson delivery system and ensuring teachers could teach it with high fidelity, we needed to determine if implementation of the model gave positive results in terms of student achievement. In the original SIOP® project, we had expected to use standardized test scores as a measure of student achievement. However, because the study preceded the NCLB legislation, most of the ELs in the districts were exempted from the districts' standardized testing process. As a result, we used the writing assessment from the Illinois Measurement of Annual Growth in English (IMAGE) test. The IMAGE was the standardized test of reading and writing that the state administrators used to measure the annual growth of these skills for ELs in grades 3 and higher. The test was valid and reliable and had correlational and predictive value for achievement scores on the IGAP (the standardized state assessment of achievement at that time for subject areas such as reading and mathematics). Our goal was to investigate English learners' performance on tasks that are critical to academic success, so we used the writing assessment as one valid measure of academic literacy.

The test called for students to write an expository essay, a task that closely approximated the academic assignments that ELs had to perform in content classrooms. The IMAGE writing rubric had a six-point scale and provided subscores for five dimensions of writing—language production, focus, support/elaboration, organization, and mechanics—as well as an overall score for each student. For each subtest, a student may have a score from zero to five; the total maximum score is twenty-five points.

During the 1998–1999 school year, we gave the IMAGE writing exam to middle school English learners in our study. A pretest was given in the fall; a posttest in the spring. Two groups of English learners in sheltered classes participated: students whose teachers were trained in implementing the SIOP® Model (the treatment group) and a similar group of English learners in the same district programs whose teachers had no exposure to the SIOP® Model (the comparison group). The students in both groups were in grades 6–8, represented mixed English proficiency levels, and spoke a variety of first languages.

Results showed that English learners in sheltered classes with teachers who had been trained in implementing the SIOP® Model improved their writing and outperformed the students in comparison classes by receiving overall higher scores for the spring assessment (Echevarria, Short, & Powers, 2006). The results for the SIOP® treatment group were statistically significant when analyzed with the comparison group for the total writing score and on three of the five subtests (language production, organization, and mechanics). The SIOP® group also made gains over the comparison group in the focus and support/elaboration subtests, but the gains were not statistically significant.

These results matched the findings from the 1997–1998 school year when a similar writing assessment requiring narrative writing was given. Furthermore, secondary analyses of the data revealed that special education students who constituted a subset of the English learners made significant improvement overall in their writing as well, with both the narrative and expository assessments. These results indicate the SIOP® Model offers a promising approach for helping English learners develop academic literacy skills needed for success in school.

Current Research on the SIOP® Model

In Chapter 8 of *Implementing the SIOP® Model through Effective Professional Development and Coaching* (Echevarria, Short, & Vogt, 2008), we describe in detail a number of empirical research studies that were taking place as of the time of that writing. This research includes program evaluation, quasi-experimental, and experimental studies that involve SIOP® professional development along with analysis of student achievement. The quasi-experimental and experimental investigations include not only subjects where the SIOP® intervention occurs but also either matched comparison subjects (teachers and students) or randomly assigned control subjects (likewise, teachers and students). Updates about many of these studies will appear on the Web sites of the SIOP® Institute (www.siopinstitute.net) and the Center for Applied Linguistics (www.cal.org/siop).

Here we'd like to share two representative studies that demonstrate the effectiveness of the SIOP® Model. The first is a program evaluation of an elementary school in Phoenix, Arizona, that implemented the SIOP® Model schoolwide, making it the sole professional development initiative for more than two years. The second is a quasi-experimental study that took place in northern New Jersey at middle and high school levels.

Lela Alston Elementary School, Isaac School District, Phoenix, Arizona

- Lela Alston initiated SIOP® professional development schoolwide in 2001. It was a new school in one of the lowest performing regions of the district. The effort was funded by a federal Title III grant for professional development.

- SIOP® professional development began when a team of seven people attended a SIOP® I Institute® in Long Beach, California. The team included district office personnel and the principal, the coach, and a third-grade teacher from Alston.

- SIOP® staff development initially took place over two years, 2002–2003 and 2003–2004. The training team—the lead SIOP® teacher, the principal, and the coach—decided to implement one component per quarter, building the teachers' cumulative knowledge of the model.

- Besides conducting whole staff trainings, the SIOP® coach and lead teacher worked with the individual teachers (e.g., observing and modeling lessons in their classrooms, helping with lesson plans) and with grade-level teams (e.g., developing a bank of language objectives for grade-level units).

- The concerted effort to train and coach all the teachers and work on grade-level lessons paid off with noteworthy gains in student achievement. Figure 3.2 below shows the student performance on the state standardized assessment, the Arizona Instrument to Measure Standards (AIMS) over three years in reading, mathematics, and writing. The 2002 student cohort averaged below 50 percent on all measures while the 2004 cohort reached close to 60 percent or above.

- In comparison with other elementary schools in the Isaac school district with similar socioeconomic status and performance levels (Esperanza, Mitchell, and PT Coe schools), Alston was more successful. At the start of SIOP® implementation, Alston students performed on par or below the students in these similar schools. By the end of three years, Alston outperformed the other schools as shown in Figure 3.3.

- Alston staff also wanted to see how students who had started at the school in kindergarten and continued through third grade performed because the school has high mobility rates and many students do not remain for all four years. Figure 3.4 shows that 86 percent of those students had met or exceeded third grade-level standards, which is remarkable for any school, especially for one with Alston's demographics.

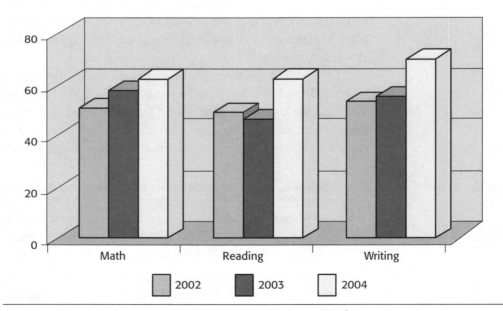

FIGURE 3.2 *Lela Alston's Grade 3 State Test Scores during SIOP® Implementation*

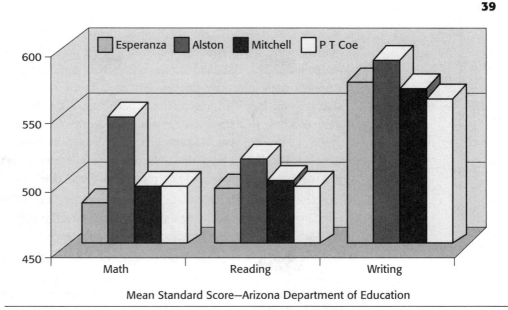

FIGURE 3.3 *Arizona's Instrument to Measure Standards, Spring 2004, Grade 3–Lela Alston School and Others*

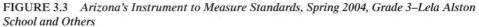

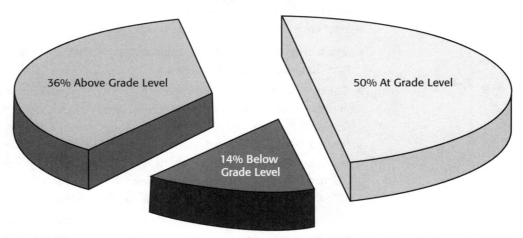

FIGURE 3.4 *Achievement of the Third-Grade Students Who Began Kindergarten at Lela Alston Elementary in the Fall of 2001*

Academic Literacy through Sheltered Instruction for Secondary English Language Learners

- This quasi-experimental research study was conducted in two districts in northern New Jersey and funded by the Carnegie Corporation of New York and the Rockefeller Foundation from 2004–2007. Both districts have two middle schools and one high school with similar multilingual English learner populations and follow an ESL program design in grades 6–12 with some designated sheltered courses. More than 500 ELs were in the treatment district (Clifton Public Schools), approximately 225 in the comparison site.

- Researchers from the Center for Applied Linguistics (CAL) provided professional development in the SIOP® Model at the treatment site. In Clifton, math, science, social studies, language arts, ESL, and technology teachers participated in SIOP® Model training. Approximately thirty-five teachers formed Cohort 1 in August 2004 and received intensive, ongoing training and occasional coaching in 2004–2005 with follow-up training and more coaching in 2005–2006. An additional twenty-five teachers formed Cohort 2 in the 2005–2006 school year and participated in the intensive training and some coaching for one year. The district supported three part-time on-site coaches in the first year and added two more in the second year to accommodate the increased size of the teacher group.

- The teachers in the comparison site did not receive any SIOP® Model training, but they continued with their regular district staff development. A total of nineteen teachers participated at the comparison site for both years.

- CAL researchers collected teacher implementation data (two classroom observations each year, one in the fall, the other in the spring) using the SIOP® protocol at both sites to assess the teachers' level of sheltered instruction. In addition, pre- and post-SIOP® lesson plans were collected at the treatment site to measure how well teachers incorporated SIOP® Model components in their preparation.

- Findings showed that the SIOP® Model Cohort 1 teachers, on average, increased their level of SIOP® implementation from fall 2004 to fall 2005 almost 20 percent as measured by the protocol. The growth was nearly the same by school level: middle school teachers improved by 20 percent on average and high school teachers by 18 percent (Short & Bauder, 2006).

- The incorporation of SIOP® features in the teachers' lesson plans improved by more than 50 percent during the first year.

- The number of high implementers of the SIOP® Model increased to a greater extent in the treatment district than the comparison district.[1] After one year of SIOP® professional development, 56 percent of Cohort 1 and 74 percent of Cohort 2 teachers in the treatment district implemented the model to a high degree. After two years, 71 percent of Cohort 1 reached a high level. In contrast, only 5 percent of the teachers reached a high level of implementation after one year at the comparison site and only 17 percent after two years (Center for Applied Linguistics, 2007).

- The researchers collected and analyzed student results on the state-approved English language proficiency assessment, the IPT (Idea Proficiency Test), for all ELs in grades 6–12. From the baseline year of 2003–2004 to Year 1 in 2004–2005 and to Year 2 in 2005–2006, analyses showed that students who had SIOP®-trained teachers in the treatment site had a statistically significant percentage growth in their mean IPT scores for the oral, reading, and writing subtests each year and from 2003–2004 to 2005–2006 (Center for Applied Linguistics, 2007).

- The researchers also collected, analyzed, and compared across the two districts student content-area achievement data from New Jersey state tests in reading, math, social studies, and science for grades 6–7[2]; reading, math, and science for grade 8;

---

[1]High implementation was determined by a score of 75 percent or higher on the SIOP® protocol. Low implementation was 50 percent or below.

[2]New Jersey changed tests during the study. In the second year, students in grades 6 and 7 were only tested in reading and math.

SIOP® coaches Alvaro Hernandez, John Seidlitz, and Amy Ditton plan a follow-up meeting for their SIOP® teacher teams.

and reading and math for grade 11 (or grade 12 for some ELs). However, the students only took these tests once, and results for subject area tests varied. In 2004–2005, Clifton SIOP® students had statistically significant results in grade 6 reading and language tests and in the total (reading + language + math) score when compared to students in the other district. The comparison students had significant results for 2004–2005 in grade 7 social studies only. In 2005–2006, Clifton SIOP® students had significant results in grade 6 language arts, grade 7 language arts, and grade 11 math. The comparison site did not have any statistically significant results when compared to Clifton that year (Center for Applied Linguistics, 2007).

The Role of the Administrator

Although teachers are the actual implementers of the SIOP® Model in the classroom, principals and other administrators play an important role in promoting high-quality sheltered instruction and supporting the teachers' delivery of it. Besides following some of the basic tenets of being an administrator in the era of school reform—hiring qualified teachers, establishing school improvement and professional development priorities, creating an educationally challenging yet supportive atmosphere, promoting inclusion and high expectations for all students–administrators need to understand what effective content-area instruction for English learners looks like. Because administrators are instructional facilitators for their school, this understanding is critical to develop. It is rarely taught in educational administration courses, and unless the administrator him- or herself has classroom experience in modifying academic instruction for ELs, it is an understanding that must be learned on the job. The SIOP® Model is the place to start.

It is important to recognize that the SIOP® Model does not require teachers to throw away their favored techniques, nor add copious new elements to a lesson. Rather, the model brings together what to teach by providing an approach for how to teach it. We recommend that school administrators use the SIOP® protocol in a checklist format when observing the lessons of new and veteran teachers. Appendix C is the SIOP® protocol modified into a checklist where an observer can record the level of implementation of the SIOP® features. An observer can note if the feature was Highly Evident, Somewhat Evident, or Not Evident in a lesson.

If the eight components are being taught to the teachers and implemented over time, then only the components already taught should be on the checklist. However, as new components are added, the checklist can grow until it represents the complete protocol. David McNeil, principal of Washington Elementary School in Phoenix, Arizona, explained what he plans to look for when he visits classes.

> A group of teachers who have taken the initiative to practice the SIOP® will come together and devise a yearly plan to outline the order of component implementation and strategies to support the implementation. For example, when we expect teachers to implement Building Background, we'll teach the four-corner vocabulary or word sort techniques across the grade levels. I will use abbreviated protocols to provide feedback on the component we are currently working with. As we add on components, the SIOP® protocol for Washington will evolve. At the end of the year, the teachers and I will use the whole protocol to provide support for student learning and engagement.

Figure 3.5 represents another observation tool that Alvaro Hernandez and colleagues in Lewisville (Texas) Independent School District (LISD) developed based on one of the SIOP® lesson plan templates (Echevarria, Vogt, & Short, 2008, p. 230). Al Hernandez,

FIGURE 3.5 *Lewisville (TX) ISD SIOP® Observation Form for Administrators*

SIOP® Observation Form for Administrators

Date:_____   Grade/Class/Subject:_____
Content Objective(s):

Language Objective(s):

Key Vocabulary   **Supplementary Materials**

SIOP® Features (check those observed)

Preparation	*Scaffolding*	*Grouping Options*
____Adaptation of content	____Modeling	____Whole class
____Links to background	____Guided practice	____Small groups
____Links to past learning	____Independent practice	____Partners
____Strategies incorporated	____Comprehensible input	____Independent

Integration of Processes	*Application*	*Assessment*
____Reading	____Hands-on	____Individual
____Writing	____Meaningful	____Group
____Speaking	____Linked to objectives	____Written
____Listening	____Promotes engagement	____Oral

Comprehensible Input
Did the students understand what they were doing and why they were doing it? Explain briefly.

Lesson Delivery
Were the students engaged approximately 90–100% of the time? Explain briefly.

who was the assistant principal at Peters Colony Elementary School and a district elementary bilingual specialist and is now a SIOP® National Faculty member, used this format as did other principals in LISD. As an alternative, you might design or modify an observation checklist to suit your district goals for staff development.

It is important to note that we designed the protocol as an observation tool, not an evaluation instrument. The protocol is best used to rate the lesson being delivered to determine how faithful it is to the full SIOP® Model. We caution administrators against using the protocol for teacher evaluation, especially while the teachers are at early stages in learning the model. In order to change their regular lesson style to the SIOP® Model, teachers must take some risks. Because the process takes time and is challenging, the lessons should not be scored for a teacher evaluation (although a coach and teacher might jointly agree to use the protocol for coaching purposes). The boxed feature offers guiding questions to consider when observing a SIOP® lesson.

The SIOP® Model offers a structure for pre-observation planning and post-observation discussion. Plus it is a means for individual teachers to reflect on how a lesson was delivered. It has also been used successfully as a guide for coaching teachers to improve their instruction, both with designated SIOP® coaches and with collaborative teams of teachers (Echevarria, Short, & Vogt, 2008).

Perhaps the most important task for a school administrator is to create a school climate where all staff have high expectations for English learners and accept responsibility for their academic achievement. By implementing the SIOP® Model schoolwide, site administrators have the opportunity to give all the teachers the skills needed to be successful with ELs in their classes, across curriculum areas.

Guiding Questions When Observing SIOP® Lessons

Lesson Preparation

Does the lesson have separate language and content objectives that are posted and discussed with students?

Are the objectives linked to the curricula or standards?

Are the content concepts suited to the grade and developmental level of the students?

Does the lesson include meaningful activities that integrate concepts with language practice?

Are supplementary materials used to support the academic text?

Building Background

Do teachers make connections between new concepts and students' personal or cultural experiences?

Do the teachers explicitly discuss prior lessons and link them to the new concepts?

Are the teachers explicitly teaching key academic vocabulary and providing multiple opportunities for ELs to use this vocabulary in meaningful ways?

Comprehensible Input

Do the teachers modulate their rate of speech, choice of words, use of idioms, and complexity of sentence structure according to the proficiency level of the English learners?

(continued)

Guiding Questions When Observing SIOP® Lessons   *(continued)*

Do the teachers explain academic tasks clearly, both orally and in writing, providing models and examples?

Does the lesson make content accessible to students through multiple ways: the use of visual aids, demonstrations, graphic organizers, vocabulary previews, predictions, cooperative learning, peer tutoring, and native language support?

Strategies

Do teachers explicitly teach study skills and learning strategies for students?

Do teachers scaffold instruction with verbal prompting (e.g., asking students to elaborate a response) and instructional tools (e.g., an outline of major topics in a chapter)?

Does the lesson incorporate higher-order questions and tasks that challenge students?

Interaction

Do lessons provide frequent opportunities for interaction and discussion between teacher and students, and among students?

Are the grouping structures appropriate to the lesson's language and content goals?

Do teachers provide sufficient wait time for students?

Do teachers allow and facilitate clarification in the native language when needed?

Practice and Application

Do lessons have hands-on practice opportunities?

Are students asked to practice and apply both the content and language skills they are learning?

Lesson Delivery

Does the lesson as implemented meet the content and language objectives?

Is the pacing appropriate for ELs? How can you tell?

Are students actively engaged throughout the class period?

Review and Assessment

Do teachers review key vocabulary and concepts at the end of the lesson?

Do teachers provide ongoing feedback to students on their work?

How does the lesson assess student learning? Are multiple options to show learning included?

Key Points Summary

- After five years of collaboration with practicing teachers, CREDE researchers developed a model of high-quality sheltered instruction known as the SIOP® Model. This model takes into account the special language development needs of English language learners, which distinguishes it from high-quality nonsheltered teaching.

- A study conducted to establish the validity and reliability of the Sheltered Instruction Observation Protocol found that the instrument is a highly reliable and valid measure of sheltered instruction (Guarino, Echevarria, Short, Schick, Forbes, & Rueda, 2001).

- Researchers compared English learners in classes whose teachers had been trained in implementing the SIOP® to a high degree to a comparison group (taught by teachers not trained in the SIOP® Model) using a prompt that required expository writing in 1998–1999. They scored the prompt using the writing rubric of the IMAGE test. The English learners in classes whose teachers had been trained in implementing the SIOP® to a high degree demonstrated significantly higher writing scores than the control group and made greater gains from the pretest to the posttest (Echevarria, Short, & Powers, 2006).

- Recent research has also shown that SIOP® Model instruction improves student language and content achievement.

- School administrators have an important role to play. They need to understand the SIOP® Model and support the teachers as they implement it in classes.

Reflect and Apply

1. Review the thirty features of the SIOP® Model from the protocol in Appendix B. Which of these do you think you understand and could recognize when well implemented in a classroom? Which ones would you need to learn more about?

2. Think about several sheltered content teachers you have observed recently. Which of the SIOP® components do they already do well? Which ones do they need to work on?

Initiating SIOP® Model Implementation in Your School or Program

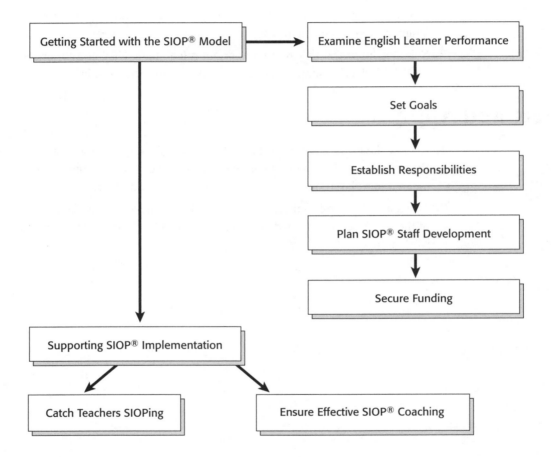

Getting Started with the SIOP® Model → Examine English Learner Performance → Set Goals → Establish Responsibilities → Plan SIOP® Staff Development → Secure Funding

Supporting SIOP® Implementation → Catch Teachers SIOPing / Ensure Effective SIOP® Coaching

Objectives

After reading, discussing, and reflecting on this chapter, you will be able to meet the following content and language objectives.

Content Objective:

Administrators will examine key elements of successful SIOP® implementation.

Language Objective:

Administrators will draft a strategic plan for implementing the SIOP® Model.

In 2001, Lela Alston Elementary School in the Isaac School District in Phoenix, Arizona, opened its doors in a poor, highly transient neighborhood with student demographics that included 97 percent of the students on free or reduced-price lunch status, 74 percent of the students identified as limited English proficient, and 10 percent with special education plans. In the spring of that school year, the principal and two teachers attended a SIOP® I Institute. They decided to make the SIOP® Model the sole professional development initiative schoolwide for the following four years. The literacy coach, Wanda Holbrook, became a full-time SIOP® coach, and a teacher, Kendra Moreno, became a part-time SIOP® trainer. They set up a professional development program for all the staff to learn the SIOP® Model over two years and the principal, Debbie Hutson, provided consistent support and leadership. Wanda, Kendra, and Debbie would meet together periodically as a committee and decide what they wanted to see with a particular component or what they wanted teachers to do. Debbie agreed, for instance, to start looking for objectives on the board and for evidence of a particular component. As she walked around the school, the teachers were very aware that she was looking to see if they were using the SIOP® Model in the classroom. They knew that she was sold on the teaching methods put forth in the protocol. She saw the value in the SIOP® Model, was supportive financially, and was willing to use the resources that were available.

Getting Started

Each site and district has approached SIOP® implementation in its own way. There is no standard set of instructions for the process, although successful implementation entails common elements. These elements include an English learner performance analysis; staff development for SIOP® teachers, coaches, and administrators; dedicated funds for the initiative; instructional leadership; coaching; course selection for students; and curriculum development. There may be unique district procedures as well, such as getting approval from the school board or involving parents in the design of a new program. The implementation process should be long term in order to generate the desired change in teacher practice and student performance, but as this chapter explores, the process can be flexible to accommodate both the resources available and the needs of the teachers and students.

Examine English Learner Performance

If you want to know where to begin, look at your data. How well are the English learners in your school or district performing? Is there a particular subject area or grade level where they are doing very well or very poorly? What has been the trend over the past few years? On average, are the students making expected progress? Or are their scores pretty much the same from year to year? If your site is like most others, the second option is more likely to be true. This is because your school or district is always receiving new beginners into the language development program while the most advanced students are exiting. As we discussed in Chapter 2, second language acquisition takes a number of years before a student can reach a proficient level on a language or content achievement measure. If the student performance is analyzed with a new group each year, the scores are likely to be fairly flat unless there has been an initiative targeting a specific skill, subject area, or group of students.

A truer measure of your program is with the former English learners. How is their performance once they have exited the language development program? Are they successful in their mainstream classes and on achievement tests? How long did it take the students who had literacy in their first language and strong educational backgrounds to exit the program? How long did it take the students who lacked native language literacy to exit?

Such analyses may reveal critical areas to start with SIOP® implementation. For instance, you may be surprised to find your students are exiting the language development program (i.e., passing the state English language proficiency test) but are not being redesignated because they cannot reach the cut-off scores on the state math and reading tests. Such a result might indicate that the language development program is not rigorous enough to prepare the students for the level of academic literacy necessary for success in the mainstream, or that the language proficiency exam is too easy, or the proficient score has been set too low.

Another scenario has the English learners meeting all the requirements for redesignation, but once they are in the mainstream classrooms, they falter. This could indicate that the mainstream teachers need support in working with former ELs. Just because students reach a minimum level of proficiency as measured by state exams, it does not mean that they cease being English learners immediately. More often these students are still developing their academic literacy skills, particularly because the complexity of language use increases with each successive grade level and academic courses become more specialized (Biancarosa & Snow, 2004; Kamil, 2003; Short & Fitzsimmons, 2007).

In a third case, we have seemingly lifelong English learners. Even after five, six, or seven years in a language development program, they aren't ready to exit. As we discussed in Chapter 1, this situation may occur if students move too often, switch program models, or have undiagnosed learning disabilities. Whichever the reason, the current program is not meeting their needs.

Set Goals for SIOP® Implementation

Once you have examined your data and considered your available and future resources, you should set some goals for SIOP® Model implementation. What would you like SIOP® instruction to change? What results would you like to see in a few years? These may be a combination of short-term and long-term goals, such as the following:

> Goal: Aim for schoolwide staff development for all teachers in a feeder cluster of schools (elementary, middle, and high) that serve a large enrollment of English learners (long term), but begin by training a smaller team of teachers in each of the three schools for the first year (short term).

Schmoker (1999, p. 31) reminds administrators that effective goals are ones that are measurable, focused on student achievement, linked to an accountability measure (so you know when you reach the goal), and written concisely in clear, direct language. Because it is important to align goals to a realistic timeline, you may spread goals (or benchmarks) over the course of several years to ensure effective and ongoing SIOP® implementation.

Establish Responsibilities

Who will lead the SIOP® implementation process at your site? A teacher leader, a designated SIOP® coach, a small team of planners? It is important to establish at least one point person to help coordinate the elements of implementation. One key aspect of this role is communication. Informing teachers about the professional development program and expectations for their involvement is critical. If outside staff developers are providing the training, then they need a consistent contact person within the school or district. If an evaluation of data is planned, then careful and timely communication among the data collectors, teachers, students, parents, and data analyzers is needed. Responsibilities may be shared among several staff members. One might become the SIOP® spokesperson who communicates with parents and others about the goals of the implementation; another might solicit funding; a third might design the staff development program and gather feedback on it.

Plan SIOP® Staff Development

One way to help our English learners is to give their teachers the tools to be successful when teaching them. Certainly one way to do this is to hire bilingual and ESL certified teachers with several years of experience teaching content-based ESL or sheltered content courses. But few administrators have the opportunity to hire a school-full of new staff, and central office administrators never do at a district level. At the time of this writing, only four states, Arizona, California, New York, and Florida, require all of their preservice teachers to study ESL methods and second language acquisition theory in order to get a teaching license. That means there are many, many teachers who do not have these foundational courses in their backgrounds and the burden falls on school districts to provide inservice training in these areas.

According to research, training teachers in the SIOP® Model is one way to offer them the tools for success (Center for Applied Linguistics, 2007; Echevarria, Short, & Powers, 2006). Organizing this staff development takes some careful consideration. Sending one teacher to a SIOP® I Institute, for example, and then expecting him or her to return to the school and train the whole staff at a faculty meeting is unrealistic. Instead, more long-term and sustained staff development should be planned. In *Implementing the SIOP® Model through Professional Development and Coaching* (Echevarria, Short, & Vogt, 2008), we share in detail the stories of sixteen schools and districts that have accomplished SIOP® implementation. All of them included sustained professional development for teachers, administrators, and other staff as part of the process.

As you plan SIOP® implementation at your site, consider the following questions as a starting point. For a more complete planning tool, see Appendix D Action Plan for SIOP® Model Implementation.

- *Who will be the first SIOP® teachers?* Select your first cohort of SIOP® teachers thoughtfully. Use your data to decide whom to invite first. It may be a grade-level team, a subject area department, or a vertical structure such as two teachers per grade so as students get promoted they will encounter trained SIOP® teachers each year.

  The group should include many good teachers who want to improve their instruction for English learners. It is helpful to have some respected teacher leaders involved as well. Be sure to mix language teachers with content teachers so the expertise of both can be brought to bear. The goal with the first cohort is to experience success with the SIOP® Model. As these teachers observe positive change in their classes, word about the value of the SIOP® Model will spread and more teachers will be eager to join in. However, do not view SIOP® staff development as a remedial, personnel improvement plan for deficient teachers.

  Marilyn Sanchez, a district administrator in Creighton, Arizona, gave this advice: "Start small and with people who really want to do it and they will be excited. One teacher told us, 'I can't believe it—the kids are actually listening!' So that success made other teachers interested in the model too."

  If this is a districtwide initiative, we encourage the participation of school teams. Teachers need support at the school level when they implement a new instructional approach like the sophisticated SIOP® Model. Having colleagues nearby to ask questions and bounce ideas around is invaluable. It is also helpful to include a site administrator on a school team.

- *What should be covered in the SIOP® staff development workshops?* Certainly, instruction on each of the eight components and thirty features of the model needs to be presented to the teachers. The period of time and length of each session will be a local decision, but we recommend two to three hours per component if possible. Some districts incorporate a summer institute with follow-up workshops during the year; others cover two components per quarter; some take two years to introduce and practice the full SIOP® Model.

  Many districts also find it valuable to address the second language acquisition process, especially if the teachers haven't had courses or workshops in this field of

Teachers and administrators attend a SIOP® workshop in South Africa.

study before. Looking at the site's student diversity and English learner performance are other topics that may be covered. In addition, as the teachers learn more of the model, some sessions might focus on lesson planning and later, curriculum development. (See Echevarria, Short, & Vogt [2008] for rich descriptions of the other districts' staff and curriculum development plans.)

Alvaro Hernandez, a former district elementary bilingual specialist and elementary school assistant principal, and a current member of the SIOP® National Faculty, offers this advice based on the SIOP® staff development program he helped establish in Lewisville (Texas) Independent School District:

Schedule SIOP® training no less than sixteen hours over eight sessions (two hours per component) and then stress to participants that this is an introduction to the model only and should be followed up with further training. Schedule SIOP® training sessions during the school year, each at least one week (preferably two) apart to allow teachers to incorporate SIOP® components into current lessons. This allows participants to reflect on their efforts. [In his district, they avoided summer sessions and consecutive day sessions.] When staff from multiple schools are involved, encourage workshops that consist of teachers from the various schools. Mixtures provide better input, focus, and less non-SIOP® personal interaction. This allows the facilitator to preserve a SIOP® focus in a low-maintenance environment.

- *When will staff development occur?* Plan for next year's training days now. Get on the school calendar as soon as possible. Claim the district professional development days for SIOP® training and look for other days to bring a cohort of SIOP® teachers together. Set aside some time in the summer before the school year begins to introduce the SIOP® Model. But avoid a five-day summer workshop without follow-up or coaching during the school year; it will *not*, in our experience, lead to change. It is better from an adult learning point of view to expect to spend about one school year introducing the eight components and thirty features to the teachers, giving them a chance to learn about the model over time and try it out in class. They should receive feedback on their SIOP® teaching and a chance to enhance what they are doing with SIOP® lessons.

Sometimes you are not ready to formalize a new staff development approach but want to introduce teachers to it, perhaps the year before full implementation. This was the situation for David McNeil, a new principal at Washington Elementary School in Phoenix, Arizona, in 2005. At that time, Washington was a low-performing school that

Washington Elementary School Faculty Meeting

David McNeil, principal of Washington Elementary School in Phoenix, Arizona, used his faculty meetings as opportunities to introduce teachers to the SIOP® Model. On early-release Wednesdays, the staff has two hours for professional development organized into three parts: 1) staff development, 2) school business, and 3) grade-level planning. They covered *Making Content Comprehensible* during the 2006–2007 year, spending two days on each chapter. An example of one meeting focusing on Comprehensible Input (CI) follows.

Staff development. After welcoming the teachers, McNeil explained the content and language objectives: "We will read about Comprehensible Input features in order to participate in a Jigsaw activity. We will explain features of Comprehensible Input orally and create a graphic organizer." He asked the teachers to do a Quickwrite on what they knew about Comprehensible Input. After two minutes, teachers shared their responses with a person from another table. For the Jigsaw activity, each teacher joined an expert group to become familiar with one of the features. Then the teachers reassembled into grade-level home groups and explained that feature to their peers. Each home group created a graphic organizer to depict the CI features. The organizers were posted, and the groups shared the information. As a wrap-up, teachers wrote one thing they could try with students to practice Comprehensible Input. Teachers were then asked to read Chapter 4 of *Making Content Comprehensible for English Learners* and try CI techniques in class.

School business. Teacher teams participated in a Graffiti Write brainstorming activity to list core beliefs and values that the school could use to improve student achievement. After two minutes, each team agreed to their top three ideas and presented them to the whole group. Together, the staff chose six statements to serve as mottos, such as "We believe all students can learn." Afterward, they discussed how the modeled cooperative learning techniques could be used to reach group consensus and facilitate presentations in their classrooms.

Grade-level planning. The final part of the meeting offered an immediate opportunity for teachers to plan lessons incorporating the modeled techniques. Grade-level teams met to accomplish this, and the principal remained available for consultation.

had experienced numerous changeovers in the school administration in prior years and consequently low staff morale. David learned about the SIOP® Model and decided to build capacity very slowly to win over the faculty. He explained his reasoning:

> I have used the SIOP® Model as a tool for planning, delivering, and assessing my staff meetings. I had a yearlong plan: every other week at faculty meetings I introduced a component and asked teachers to read the chapter, practice implementing the component, and discuss challenges and successes. We repeated this process, modeling content and language objectives, modeling instructional and learning strategies to encourage teachers to use the SIOP®. I did not mandate teachers use the SIOP® Model in the 2006–2007 school year, but after a year of modeling and providing feedback using terminology from the SIOP® protocol, I expect that next year we will establish a timeline to implement a component at a time using strategies that will support teachers' implementation, inquiries, and concerns.

- *How can more teachers be added to the SIOP® training?* Once the first cohort has participated in SIOP® staff development, it is beneficial to add teachers to the SIOP® team. Some districts, like Clifton Public Schools (New Jersey), have added a new cohort each year. Others, like Lewisville Independent School District (Texas), add a new group each semester. Charlotte-Mecklenburg Schools (North Carolina) brings on new school teams each year.

  It is useful to select the next cohort of teachers strategically. Ask yourself which subjects or grades need the most support in future years. For example, if ninth-grade teachers representing various sheltered high school course subjects were included in the first cohort, the next cohort might include tenth-grade teachers of the next level of sheltered courses so as the students move up the grades, they will encounter teachers trained (or being trained) in the SIOP® Model.

  It is also very important to plan for staff turnover. For a variety of reasons, teachers come and go in schools. A teacher you may have invested in with SIOP® training may leave the next school year. Therefore it is useful to have a process for accommodating new and replacement teachers on the SIOP® team. Some schools, such as Lela Alston Elementary School in Phoenix, partner new teachers with experienced SIOP® educators and provide some after-school sessions to introduce them to the model. (Of course, when interviewing potential candidates, the principal informs them they would need to attend professional development and become SIOP® teachers.)

- *Besides teachers, who needs SIOP® staff development?* A serious goal is schoolwide SIOP® implementation. Therefore, all staff should have SIOP® training in time. A staff knowledgeable about ELs will make more informed decisions about students, their placement, schedules, and academic plans.

  1. If there will be one or more SIOP® Coaches, those educators need general SIOP® training and training in SIOP® coaching (such as at a SIOP® II Institute).

  2. School-level administrators—principals, assistant principals, and department chairs—need to have a basic understanding of the SIOP® Model and how they can support implementation.

  3. Other school specialists, such as special education, reading, and gifted and talented specialists, need targeted preparation for assessing and working with ELs, especially as they are called on more and more to serve these students.

4. School counselors need to be included. Joan Rolston of Charlotte-Mecklenburg Schools has developed a special training just for counselors to help them understand the second language acquisition process, plan sheltered courses in secondary schools and schedule ELs appropriately, and more. As she points out, "Counselors must be kept in the loop—they are always looking through the lenses of overall student success and graduation requirements." See the boxed feature on the opposite page for a list of the five top professional development topics she recommends for guidance counselors.

Secure Funding for Sustained SIOP® Implementation

While funding a school- or districtwide initiative may take some time to arrange, the cost need not be insurmountable and SIOP® implementation can begin on a small scale if necessary. The following steps should be useful in stimulating your planning.

1. Determine the purposes for the funds designated for SIOP® implementation. Broad categories include coaching, professional development, assessment and program evaluation, and materials. Figure 4.1 is a checklist of common uses of SIOP® funds that can help you determine your expenses.

FIGURE 4.1   *Checklist of SIOP® Funding Purposes*

___ Teacher stipends (for professional development or curriculum development outside of school hours)
___ Professional development materials
___ Substitute fees for teachers (for peer observations or for workshops during school hours)
___ Professional development consultants
___ Salary for coaches
___ Supplies for coaching
___ Student instructional materials (e.g., supplementary readers, math manipulatives)
___ SIOP®-focused curriculum development
___ Assessment data collection and analysis
___ Travel to conferences, other districts for observations, and other professional development venues
___ Other:_____

2. Consider all possible funding sources, current and future. Figure 4.2 is a chart that you can complete, reflecting your local and state circumstances. You will notice that federal, state, and local funds are major sources, but philanthropic organizations, large corporations, local businesses, and partnerships should also be considered. Most districts that

FIGURE 4.2   *Sources of SIOP® Funding*

Federal Funds and Grants	State Funds and Grants	Foundations and Other Philanthropies	Corporations and Large Businesses	Potential/Future Partners
Title I (for disadvantaged students)	Professional development funds	Education-oriented foundations	Local corporations with tax incentives	University-district partnerships
Title IIa (for teacher development)	English learner funds			
Title III (for English language acquisition)	School improvement			
Emergency Immigrant				

Top Five Professional Development Topics
for Guidance Counselors Serving English Learners

1. **No Child Left Behind (NCLB)**—Counselors need to know how NCLB regulations affect English learners, in terms of course scheduling and testing. Content area teachers have important roles with these students. ESL teachers have somewhat different roles focusing on English language development courses and also requiring more collaboration with content area teachers. Counselors should be reminded that all students deserve "equal opportunity and access to curriculum and instruction."

2. **Diversity among English Learners**—Counselors need a firm grounding in the backgrounds of the diverse youth in their schools. They must understand that not all the ELs are alike and should not have cookie-cutter schedules. They should spend time with an initial interview (and any data they receive from an intake center with diagnostic test results) to determine as best they can a student's educational background, first language literacy skill, educational aspirations, and course interests. They also need to realize that there are different kinds of English learners. A low proficiency level in the English language does not always mean a low level of content area knowledge. Counselors must separate a student's language development needs from his or her content area needs. In this way, counselors can fully understand how a student will progress through the educational experience and the second language acquisition process and can plan a pathway through high school, for example, accordingly.

3. **Second Language Acquisition**—Coupled with the awareness of student diversity, counselors need to understand how one learns a new language, which factors might inhibit or accelerate the learning process, how long it might take, and so on. [Information provided in Chapter 2 is critical for addressing this topic.] In addition, for high schoolers who have considerably less time to become academically literate in the new language and master all the required courses for graduation, counselors might seek out opportunities for students to extend the time available for learning English (such as after-school, Saturday, and summer courses).

4. **The SIOP® Model**—A general overview of the SIOP® Model is critical for counselors. They need a basic understanding of the eight components and thirty features and the value the model offers to student learning. This knowledge allows counselors to see the significance of ensuring that ELs are scheduled with SIOP®-trained teachers and how they (the counselors) fit into the educational process without being involved in the actual classroom instruction.

5. **State and Local Requirements**—Counselors benefit from knowing the big picture for these learners, especially regarding courses required for promotion and graduation. A staff development session can help counselors understand how the SIOP® Model "fits" into these requirements and the potential positive impact of SIOP® instruction for the English learners.

Joan Rolston, ESL-Second Language Department, Charlotte-Mecklenburg Schools have implemented the SIOP® Model have commingled funds from a variety of sources in order to best serve the English learners and meet the requirements of NCLB.

3. Clearly allocate the funds to the SIOP® implementation process. Dedicated funding that endures over time is needed to ensure effective implementation. Be very cautious of competing initiatives that may crop up and seek to draw monies (as well as teachers' time and effort) from the SIOP® funds. You are making an investment in the SIOP® Model and need to provide the time and attention for several years so the positive effects on English learner achievement can occur.

4. Align the budget (amount secured + expected to secure over time) with the implementation plan. Here is the place to be realistic and make sure that sufficient resources are allocated for each element of the plan and spread out over a time frame that will permit sustained implementation.

Supporting SIOP® Implementation

Catch Teachers SIOPing

When teachers and staff take on a new, long-term initiative, administrative support is paramount. Not only do we want the principals to understand what the SIOP® Model sets out to accomplish in terms of teacher practice and student performance, we want them to know what to look for when they enter SIOP® classrooms. As instructional leaders, our administrators should be able to engage with the teachers about the lessons. For example, they should be able to discuss the merits of activities that support language and content learning; help grade-level or content-area teams identify cross-curricular objectives, standards, and techniques; and explore ways that teachers can reduce the language load of some classroom assessments.

While we do not encourage principals or assistant principals to use the SIOP® protocol to evaluate the teachers, especially as they are learning the model and may be tentative with some lesson techniques, administrators do need to know which features to look for in SIOP® classrooms. Furthermore, if the administrators and staff share a common SIOP® lexicon, they can have robust conversations about effective instruction. A principal doing a walk-through might look for posted language and content objectives and listen for evidence that the objectives are being supported by the lesson activities. A coach might sit down to give feedback to a teacher and discuss better ways he or she might have built background or encouraged elaborated student responses in the observed lesson.

When asked how he plans to give feedback to teachers who are beginning to implement the SIOP® Model, David McNeil, principal of Washington Elementary School in Phoenix, replied,

> I enjoy celebrating teacher innovations and look forward to creating multiple arenas where we are acknowledging teachers' implementation of the SIOP® Model. I want to create an "I caught you . . . SIOPing" board and place photos of teachers posting objectives, using word walls, conga lines, and so forth. I would like teachers to share SIOP® successes at staff meetings and encourage teachers who have visited other teachers during their planning time to praise what they observed in colleagues' classrooms. My coaches and I will provide feedback to teachers using the protocol and focus on using the terminology in the SIOP® Model to improve communication and create a consistency in teaching expectations across classroom boundaries.

Ensure Effective SIOP® Coaching

School administrators intending to incorporate SIOP® coaching in their implementation plan need to realize that staffing a SIOP® Coach position is not an easy process. Administrators should select a coach carefully and arrange for ongoing professional development on coaching for that individual. Learning to be an effective SIOP® Coach takes time, sensitivity, knowledge, and practice. Working effectively with teachers who are learning to implement the SIOP® Model involves building trust and sharing a commitment (Sherris, 2007). Therefore, administrators want to choose a coach who enjoys working as part of a team and readily conveys respect to colleagues. It is most important to remember that the SIOP® Coach's role is to mentor the teachers, to facilitate their learning of this new approach, and to support them in the ups and downs of implementation. The SIOP® Coach should not evaluate the teachers in any formal way. The boxed feature lists some characteristics of SIOP® Coaches.

In planning SIOP® coaching, administrators will want to consider the personalities and abilities of the individuals involved. The relationship between the coach and teacher may be one of expert-novice or of equal partners. In the former case, the coach is often an experienced SIOP® implementer and coach, and the teacher is just beginning to learn

What a SIOP® Coach IS and Is NOT

What a SIOP® Coach IS

- A SIOP® Coach is a facilitator, mentor, and advisor.

- A variety of educational specialists can become SIOP® Coaches, such as a 1) district-level coach or staff development specialist, 2) site facilitator, 3) teacher mentor, 4) lead ESL teacher, 5) peer teacher, or 6) external staff developer.

- An effective SIOP® Coach has a high level of knowledge about

  o the SIOP® Model;

  o second language acquisition;

  o the established curricula of the courses where SIOP® lessons are being implemented; and

  o coaching and mentoring adults.

- A SIOP® Coach has experience as a professional developer.

- Ideally, a SIOP® Coach has already taught using the SIOP® Model. Such a background validates the relationship between coach and teacher because the coach will have experienced the effort it takes to become a SIOP® teacher and can more readily relate to challenges and successes a new SIOP® teacher may have.

What a SIOP® Coach Is NOT

- A SIOP® Coach is not an evaluator.

- A SIOP® Coach should not have direct supervisory responsibility for the teachers.

- A SIOP® Coach is not a literacy coach, reading specialist, ESL teacher, or any other educator with just a new label added on to his or her job description.

about the SIOP® Model. In the latter, teacher colleagues may be coaching one another as they implement the model in their classes. In some cases, an ESL teacher and a content or grade-level classroom teacher may work together as peer coaches. But it is crucial for the coach to have the respect of the teachers and be able to gain their trust. Together the administrators, coaches, and teachers must build a culture of mutual support and collaboration (Bauder, 2007).

The following guidelines delineate the professional knowledge and experience required of SIOP® Coaches. More details are found in *Implementing the SIOP® Model* (Echevarria, Short, & Vogt, 2008).

- **Deep knowledge of the SIOP® Model.** The coach needs to be well versed in the theory and research that support the model and must understand what high-quality SIOP® instruction looks like in a variety of classrooms and subject areas. The best knowledge can be gained by a combination of experiences: reading research on the SIOP® Model, observing in SIOP® classrooms, writing SIOP® lessons, and teaching with the SIOP® Model.

- **Knowledge of second language acquisition theory and literacy development for children and adolescents.** To help teachers, coaches need to convey how second language learning occurs, which individual characteristics and sociocultural factors affect second language development, and how it differs from first language development. Coaches must be able to show teachers how literacy can be fostered through content area instruction, both initial literacy (learning to read) and academic literacy (reading to learn).

- **Knowledge of ESL methods.** The SIOP® Coach must work with the teachers to incorporate content-based ESL and sheltered instruction techniques in their lessons. Although the SIOP® Model offers teachers flexibility in the activities they include in lessons, not all will be familiar with ESL methods nor know which ones are the best to use in a given situation. As a result, they will look to the coach for training and guidance. The coach will find *99 Ideas and Activities for Teaching with the SIOP® Model* (Vogt & Echevarria, 2008) to be a valuable resource in this effort.

- **Basic understanding of the content area curricula.** In order to help teachers design lessons and plan objectives, general knowledge of the content area curricula is indispensable. The SIOP® Coach need not know everything about all subjects he or she supports but should know the gist of the main topics and be able to identify the language patterns and structures used in the different subjects.

- **Leadership skills.** The SIOP® Coach must be a leader, because he or she is guiding teachers along a path of new knowledge. This path may have some rough spots, and strong leadership skills will help the teachers stay the course, maintain focus, and reach their goals.

- **Coaching/mentoring experience.** The SIOP® Coach should already have experience as a successful coach or teacher mentor. The coach may employ a feedback process, such as the cognitive coaching approach (Costa & Garmston, 2002) to understand a teacher's thought processes (while planning and delivering SIOP® lessons) and encourage teacher reflection.

When Charlotte-Mecklenburg Schools (CMS) decided to hire a full-time SIOP® Coach after one year of implementation, the district used these guidelines to describe the

FIGURE 4.3 *SIOP® Coach: Charlotte-Mecklenburg Job Announcement*

JOB TITLE: *Sheltered Instruction (SIOP®) Coach*   DEPARTMENT: *High School*
DATE: January 11, 2005   *Curriculum and Instruction*

Responsibilities/Duties/Tasks:

- Participate in the implementation of Title III of NCLB by providing high-quality, on-going staff development in sheltered instruction
- Coach SIOP®-trained teachers through site visits, coplanning, e-mail, and site-based SIOP® follow-up support meetings
- Participate in the selection and development of curricular materials for sheltered instruction classes (e.g., create model lessons)
- Demonstrate model lessons for classroom and content-area teachers using sheltered instruction techniques
- Represent Charlotte-Mecklenburg Schools on the Dept. of Public Instruction (DPI) committee to develop the North Carolina SIOP® Model
- Maintain communication with SIOP®-trained teachers through class visits, meetings, and e-mail
- Coordinate with all content specialists to plan for SIOP® training and materials selection
- Collaborate with the ESL-Second Language Department to plan and deliver staff development
- Provide feedback to teachers, principals, and assistant principals
- Respond to phone calls from teachers and administrators
- Attend and conduct workshops on the local, state, and national level
- Host delegations from other districts and DPI to disseminate sheltered instruction program successes

Other Requirements:

- Must be able to work collaboratively within and across departments
- Must be able to implement and monitor best practices in second language acquisition
- Must value diversity and possess the ability to develop programs to meet the needs of linguistically and culturally diverse populations
- Must be proficient in the use of Microsoft Office products (e.g., Word, Excel, PowerPoint)
- Must have excellent written and verbal skills

Expertise	*Minimum*	*Desirable*
A. Education	*Possession of or ability to obtain NC ESL certification*	*Master's degree in ESL, or applied linguistics*
B. Experience/Training (Type and Length)	*Three years successful teaching experience with second language learners*	*Two to five years of administrative or lead/resource teacher experience; experience in training staff on strategies for English language learners including the SIOP® Model*

position. You may find the CMS job announcement in Figure 4.3 useful as you move forward with coaching as well.

Once you have selected the SIOP® Coach and ensured initial training, the next task is to support the coaching process. To do so, you must give the coach time and resources to be an effective guide to the new SIOP® teachers. Liz Warner, the elementary ESL specialist in Washoe County Schools in Reno, Nevada, and a SIOP® National Faculty member, explained the situation in her district where this was not planned for:

Our biggest problem here is follow-up. You have ninety-one schools in your district and you have a total of two trainers that can do follow-up during the school day. The other trainers are classroom teachers, so you have to sub them out in order for them to be able to do follow-up. I think that the biggest challenge with any kind of professional development program is follow-up. And if the principal doesn't know how to follow up, it's a problem.

Time for coaching. For coaching to be effective, appropriate time slots need to be secured in the instructional landscape. This requires a commitment on the administration's part because the school day is already heavily parceled out. It is easier when the SIOP® Coach has a full-time position, rather than a part-time one, because the coach can focus exclusively on SIOP® instruction. However, many districts begin with a part-time coach for fiscal reasons, yet that decision poses challenges for scheduling and prioritizing activities. In one district, the administration selected three high school ESL SIOP® teachers to support implementation among thirty teachers at their school. Each coach was asked to devote her duty period to SIOP® coaching, but with a full teaching load, it was difficult for each to mentor her ten teachers equally. If an assigned teacher did not have a class during the coach's duty period, it was hard to conduct observations.

Therefore, in order for the SIOP® Coach to observe teachers, both the teacher and coach need some release time to accommodate a preobservation meeting and a postobservation conference. The coach furthermore needs time to make the observations. When the coach wants to meet with a team of SIOP® teachers, it is most helpful for administrators to schedule those meetings at times convenient for the members, ideally during the regular school hours.

Time for learning. Just as coaches need time set aside to accomplish their tasks, teachers need dedicated time for learning about the SIOP® Model. Administrators can consult with coaches and the staff to set up one or more of the contexts described below.

- **SIOP® Study Group.** The SIOP® Coach convenes a group of teachers interested in the SIOP® Model, usually for after-school meetings, to read and discuss *Making Content Comprehensible for English Learners: The SIOP® Model* (Echevarria, Vogt, & Short, 2008). The teachers try implementing features of the model and report back at future meetings.

- **SIOP® Team Planning.** SIOP® team members have joint planning time with coaches. The members help one another plan lessons, and the coach may also demonstrate sheltered techniques. The administration of the school must protect these planning periods. In other words, special meetings like special education referrals should not be scheduled at this time, and interruptions should be minimized.

- **SIOP® Professional Learning Community (PLC).** A SIOP® PLC may begin as a small team of teachers, SIOP® Coach, and administrators in a school but grow into a schoolwide approach after a few years. Membership should be voluntary with teachers who have at least two years of teaching experience. The purpose of the SIOP® PLC may shift over time as the implementation process matures (Hord, 1997). For example, one purpose might be to support the teachers who are beginning to implement the model. In later years, the purpose might shift to curriculum development, where SIOP® language objectives and teaching techniques are embedded in sheltered content courses.

- **SIOP® Lesson Study.** A group of SIOP® teachers codevelop a lesson in response to a research question they have generated that is tied to a student learning goal (Lewis, 2002). One teacher in the group teaches the lesson while the others observe. They regroup and may revise the lesson. If so, another teacher teaches it and the rest observe. After about two cycles, the lesson is finalized and made available to other teachers.

- **SIOP® Critical Friends Group.** SIOP® teachers convene once each month to examine student work using a specific protocol (Bambino, 2002; Cushman, 1998). The group is led by a trained facilitator who guides the process. One teacher per session usually presents his or her students' work, group members critique, and the teacher reflects. The group usually sets a goal for improving student learning and identifies some strategies for teachers to implement, in this case using the SIOP® Model.

- **Peer SIOP® Observations and Coaching.** SIOP® teachers may observe one another as a means for seeing the SIOP® Model in action. It is often helpful for teachers new to the SIOP® Model to see how others deliver their lessons, especially if some of the teachers they observe are more experienced. In some cases, SIOP® teachers may act as peer coaches. To do so successfully they need a specific purpose for the observation (e.g., watch for use of higher-order questions), and some guidance in the best way to share observations with their peers (e.g., with nonevaluative comments). A teacher may also videotape a lesson and review it with a "critical friend." This condition should not replace coaching with a trained SIOP® Coach, but may be an additional support.

Key Points Summary

- Look at your English learner performance for the past few years and decide a focal area for implementation activities. Take account of current resources, trained personnel, and funding opportunities.

- Set a SIOP® implementation goal. Decide what should happen and what the expected result should be in the short term and long term.

- Determine the point person for SIOP® implementation and that person's responsibilities. Consider forming a support team. Be realistic about what can be accomplished in the short term given available resources and competing initiatives. Plan for ongoing, long-term implementation.

- Identify strategic cohorts of teachers to receive SIOP® training and organize staff development on the eight components and thirty features of the SIOP® Model as well as other key topics. Work with the staff developers on a sustained program for the teachers, providing time for teacher learning and reflection. Avoid competing initiatives.

- Select a SIOP® Coach with the appropriate background and experience to support job-embedded SIOP® training and focused implementation in the classroom. Be sure the coach has adequate time in his or her schedule to mentor the teachers.

Reflect and Apply

1. After reading this chapter, what is your initial plan for supporting SIOP® implementation? How many teachers will be in the first training cohort? Who will be the point person for the process? What is one short-term and one long-term SIOP® goal?

2. Think of the personnel in your school or district. Who comes to mind as an excellent candidate for becoming a SIOP® Coach? What should be the key elements of the SIOP® Coach's job description?

chapter 5

Restructuring Your School or Program with the SIOP® Model

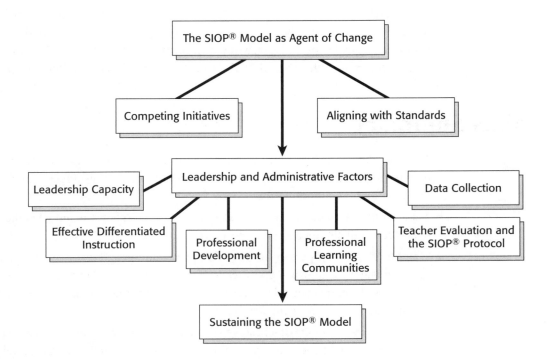

The SIOP® Model as Agent of Change

Competing Initiatives

Aligning with Standards

Leadership and Administrative Factors

Leadership Capacity

Data Collection

Effective Differentiated Instruction

Professional Development

Professional Learning Communities

Teacher Evaluation and the SIOP® Protocol

Sustaining the SIOP® Model

Objectives

After reading, discussing, and reflecting on this chapter, you will be able to meet the following content and language objectives.

Content Objectives:

Administrators will evaluate various approaches for introducing and implementing the SIOP® Model in schools and districts.

Administrators will examine approaches for sustainability of the SIOP® Model over time.

Language Objectives:

Administrators will be able to explain how to use the SIOP® protocol for observation, conferencing, and collaborative discussion with teachers and support staff.

Administrators will describe differentiated and non-differentiated classroom structures and compare those to existing structures in their own schools.

Look around. Listen as the noisy swarm of students becomes quiet when the bell rings and students and teachers move into classrooms, with doors closing behind them. What's happening behind those doors? What are students learning? How are teachers teaching? How often should you open those doors and enter, or should you mostly stay away? How do you discover what is really going on between the teacher and the students? What recognition can you give to teachers who are already excelling, or what assistance can you give to those who are floundering or who are simply making it through each year? What can you do, as only one person, with responsibilities for a teaching staff of 125 or 25 or 7 in a school? As an administrator, you are bombarded with so many student needs, parent worries, teacher concerns, district and state initiatives, and paperwork that it seems futile to think of improving the teaching of every teacher, much less restructuring your entire school. What indeed can one person do?

It is no surprise that school leadership is incredibly challenging. With an increased focus on school accountability, standards-based instruction, and high-stakes testing, developing meaningful ways to reframe and refocus a school for excellence may feel like just one more priority to address, among all of the others. However, when there are students whose academic needs are not being met, and these students are arriving at our school doors in ever-increasing numbers, some changes need to be made.

Using the SIOP® Model to Organize for Change

In the previous chapter, we discussed issues of getting started with implementation of the SIOP® Model and the administrator's role in facilitating professional development for teachers of English learners. In this chapter, we suggest that the SIOP® Model can also serve as a framework to organize for change. In an era of unprecedented educational reform, schools and districts are undertaking untold numbers of initiatives, with thousands of schools and districts also attempting to respond to calls for school improvement (Goldenberg, 2004). We all realize we can no longer do business as usual in schools and expect different results, especially for English learners. However, when reform efforts and initiatives compete with each other for funding, leadership, and time, administrators and their staff can become frustrated easily and overwhelmed.

Reducing Competing Initiatives

As teachers and administrators become knowledgeable about and committed to the SIOP® Model as a means for improving the academic achievement of English learners, they realize that the model is not simply another new "program." Rather, it can serve as an organizational framework for bringing together a variety of effective instructional methods and practices.

The SIOP® Model was scientifically validated by the systematic and consistent use of the thirty features described in Chapter 3. These features, including teaching to objectives, focusing on vocabulary development, explaining academic tasks in a clear fashion, explicitly teaching learning strategies, asking higher-order questions, grouping students to achieve differentiated instruction, and assessing student comprehension throughout a lesson, are but a few aspects of the SIOP® Model that are found in many other approaches to teaching and learning. Thus, the SIOP® Model offers a way to consolidate the features of effective instruction, making it compatible with a variety of methods and approaches associated with current reform efforts.

For example, many U.S. schools have been designated as Reading First schools, and as such they are required to provide explicit, effective instruction in literacy with the goal of improving reading ability. A number of schools have included the SIOP® Model as part of their professional development plans for Reading First because the features of the model are so congruent with effective literacy instruction for young children. Note the following SIOP® features that are also considered essential for the literacy development of young children:

- Explicit connections made between content concepts and students' backgrounds
- Focused attention on vocabulary development and instruction
- Structured opportunities for children to engage in language use and interaction with other students and the teacher
- The teaching of cognitive and metacognitive reading and learning strategies
- Assessment of student comprehension.

In another example, most if not all U.S. school districts have designed curriculum around state content standards. Adherence to the SIOP® Model requires a daily focus on

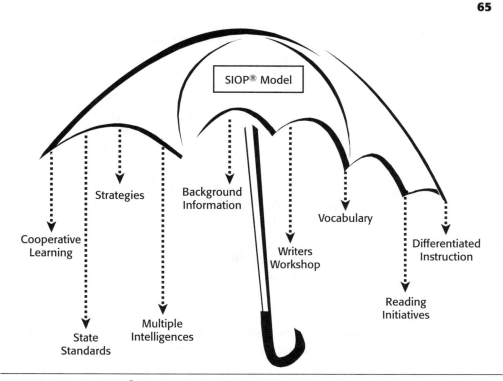

FIGURE 5.1 *The SIOP® Framework for Organizing Instruction*

writing, posting, and explaining to students both content and language objectives, which are in large part derived from district curricula and state standards.

We can take most current initiatives and reform efforts and situate them within the SIOP® Model, such as multiple intelligences, differentiated instruction, cooperative learning, Professional Learning Communities (PLCs), and so forth. We often think of the SIOP® Model as an umbrella under which the other initiatives and reform efforts reside (see Figure 5.1).

As you begin discussing the SIOP® Model with your staff, parents, district administrators, school board, and other stakeholders, it might be helpful to match your school's current initiatives and/or standards with the features of the SIOP® Model and create your own school or district umbrella. As we all know, one of the biggest challenges to any new initiative is resistance from those teachers and administrators who think

1. We've been there/done that;
2. If we wait long enough, this will go away; or
3. This is one more new thing on our plates . . . what can we now remove?

If we help educators understand that the SIOP® Model can coordinate the other initiatives instructionally and is not the newest, greatest "program" in education that will soon be replaced by another, there is less resistance and more buy-in from the start. We have heard repeatedly from SIOP® teachers that once they developed an understanding of how the SIOP® Model better organized what they were already doing, they were greatly relieved that they didn't have to abandon teaching practices they knew were effective (Echevarria, Short, & Vogt, 2008).

Aligning the SIOP® Model with District and State Standards

Because the SIOP® Model was originally validated with English learners in sheltered content classrooms, some educators believe it is only for "those" students and "those" teachers. However, in reality, in many classrooms throughout the United States, English learners are interspersed with native English speakers, and this necessitates that all teachers who have ELs (or former ELs who have been redesignated) in their classrooms must learn how to effectively teach them. Moreover, a focus on academic literacy can be extremely valuable for a wide variety of students, ELs and non-ELs alike.

To further illustrate that the SIOP® Model is compatible with district initiatives and standards, we offer an example from the Charlotte-Mecklenburg Schools (CMS), which has implemented the SIOP® Model in more than thirty pilot schools across K–12 ESL and sheltered classrooms for the past few years. CMS has provided SIOP® professional development for many administrators and teachers, who then help train the other teachers in their schools. In general, a new team of teachers per school is trained each year. This represents a major, systemic change for the school district in order to meet the academic needs of the ever-increasing numbers of English learners.

To integrate the SIOP® Model with district policies in 2007, Ivanna Mann Thrower, the district SIOP® Coach, and Jennifer Lupold Pearsall, the second language specialist from the ESL-Second Language Department, created a correlation between SIOP® features and the district's evaluation form, the TPAI-R (Teacher Performance Appraisal Instrument-Revised) (see Figure 5.2). This chart has helped teachers and administrators

FIGURE 5.2 *SIOP® Correlation to Teacher Performance Appraisal Instrument-Revised (TPAI-R, Charlotte-Mecklenburg Schools)*

SIOP® Model Components	TPAI-R Indicators	
Lesson Preparation		
1. Write *content objectives* clearly for students.	3.12	Students engaged, responsible for learning
2. Write *language objectives* clearly for students.		
3. Choose *content concepts appropriate* for age and educational background level of students.	3.9 6.1	Adapts instruction to diverse learners Aligned instructional plans
4. Identify *supplementary materials* to use (graphs, models, visuals).	3.4 3.11	Relevant examples Uses technology to support instruction
5. *Adapt content* (e.g., text, assignment) to all levels of student proficiency.	3.9	Adapts instruction to diverse learners
6. Plan *meaningful activities* that integrate lesson concepts (e.g., surveys, letter writing, simulations, constructing models) with language practice opportunities for reading, writing, listening, and/or speaking.	3.9	Adapts instruction to diverse learners
Building Background		
7. *Explicitly link concepts* to students' backgrounds and experiences.	1.3 3.4	Time on task for learning Relevant examples
8. *Explicitly link past learning* and new concepts.	3.1 3.4	Links to prior learning Relevant examples
9. *Emphasize key vocabulary* (e.g., introduce, write, repeat, and highlight) for students.	3.4	Relevant examples

FIGURE 5.2 *(Continued)*

SIOP® Model Components	TPAI-R Indicators

Comprehensible Input

10. Use *speech* appropriate for students' proficiency level (e.g., slower rate, enunciation, and simple sentence structure for beginners).

    3.3   Speaks fluently
    3.6   Brisk pace, slowing when necessary

11. *Explain academic tasks* clearly.

    3.8   Assignment clear

12. Use a *variety of techniques* to make content concepts clear (e.g., modeling, visuals, hands-on activities, demonstrations, gestures, body language).

    3.4   Relevant examples

Strategies

13. Provide ample opportunities for students to use *learning strategies* (e.g., problem solving, predicting, organizing, summarizing, categorizing, evaluating, self-monitoring).

    3.5   High rate of success on tasks

14. Use *scaffolding techniques* consistently (providing the right amount of support to move students from one level of understanding to a higher level) throughout lesson.

15. Use a variety of *question types including those that promote higher-order thinking* skills throughout the lesson (e.g., literal, analytical, and interpretive questions).

    3.5   High rate of success on tasks

Interaction

16. Provide frequent *opportunities for interactions* and discussion between teacher/student and among students, and encourage elaborated responses.

    1.3   Time on task for learning
    3.12 Students engaged, responsible for learning

17. Use *group configurations* that support language and content objectives of the lesson.

    3.9   Adapts instruction to diverse learners

18. Provide sufficient *wait time for student responses* consistently.

    4.4   Questions, clear, one at a time

19. Give ample opportunities for *students to clarify key concepts in L1* as needed with aide, peer, or L1 text.

    3.5   High rate of success on tasks

Practice/Application

20. Provide *hands-on materials* and/or manipulatives for students to practice using new content knowledge.

    1.3   Time on task for learning
    3.12 Students engaged, responsible for learning

21. Provide activities for students to *apply content and language knowledge* in the classroom.

    3.5   High rate of success on tasks

22. Provide activities that *integrate all language skills* (i.e., reading, writing, listening, and speaking).

    6.1   Aligned instructional plans

Lesson Delivery

23. *Support content objectives* clearly.

    3.12 Students engaged, responsible for learning
    6.1   Aligned instructional plans

24. *Support language objectives* clearly.

25. *Engage students* approximately 90–100% of the period (most students taking part and on task throughout the lesson).

    1.3   Time on task for learning

26. *Pace* the lesson appropriately to the students' ability level.

    3.9   Adapts instruction to diverse learners

Review/Assessment

27. Give a comprehensive *review of key vocabulary*.

    4.3   Uses oral, written, and other work products to check progress

28. Give a comprehensive *review of key content concepts*.

    4.3   Uses oral, written, and other work products to check progress

29. Provide *feedback* to students regularly on their output (e.g., language, content, work).

    5.1   Feedback on in-class work
    5.2   Prompt feedback on out-of-class work
    5.3   Affirms correct response quickly

30. Conduct *assessments* of student comprehension and learning throughout lesson on all lesson objectives (e.g., spot checking, group response).

    4.3   Uses oral, written, and other work products to check progress understand how the SIOP® Model operationalizes the district teacher performance standards and once again reinforces the notion that most of the SIOP® features are familiar; and many are already being included in teachers' lessons. (For more information about how CMS has implemented the SIOP® Model, see Echevarria, Short, & Vogt, 2008).

Leadership and Administrative Factors

Several other important factors should be considered from a leadership and administrative standpoint before adopting the SIOP® Model for schoolwide use. They include

- leadership capacity;
- the role of the administrator in professional development related to the SIOP® Model;
- the role of Professional Learning Communities and/or staff collaboration;
- data collection;
- use of the SIOP® protocol for teacher evaluation; and
- effective differentiated instruction.

Leadership Capacity

With any reform effort, a school leader must solicit and attract a critical mass of teachers to support the overall notion of restructuring a school toward excellence. Building leadership capacity, where most teachers and support faculty become instructional leaders, is crucial (Lambert, 1998, p. 89).

Five assumptions serve as a basis for building leadership capacity:

- *Leadership* may be provided by those who are not necessarily considered *leaders*; *leadership* and *leader* are not the same.
- Leadership is about learning.
- Everyone has the potential and right to work as a leader.
- Leading is a shared endeavor.
- Leadership requires the redistribution of power and authority.

Using the above assumptions as a foundational framework, administrators then need to consider the following factors when restructuring a school so that staff will be poised to implement a new or different curricular or instructional focus:

1. Hire personnel with the capacity to do leadership work;
2. Get staff to know one another;
3. Assess staff and school capacity for leadership;
4. Develop a culture of inquiry;
5. Organize the school community for leadership work;

6. Implement plans for building leadership capacity;

7. Develop district policies and practices that support leadership capacity building (adapted from Lambert, 1998).

The Role of Professional Development: The School Leader's Participatory Role

When choosing the SIOP® Model as an organizational and restructuring tool, professional development becomes an integral part of the entire implementation experience. Steeped in collaboration among administrators, teachers, and support staff, all become well versed in the multiple dimensions of the SIOP® Model and its many uses.

Therefore, training and professional development do not begin and end with the teachers. Administrators also need to be educated in the SIOP® Model and the issues associated with its implementation. The more collaborative the process (implementing the SIOP® Model), the more likely the chance for success (see Echevarria, Short, & Vogt, 2008, for detailed examples). In order for effective school restructuring to occur, all school site educators need an in-depth understanding of each of the SIOP® components and how the entire model can be used to improve teaching and learning.

Typically, teachers are taught and coached by trainers in how to carry out new programs, reform techniques, and curriculum. Sustained and consistent implementation among all teachers, with support by all administrators, is necessary for success. How then does the SIOP® Model's sustainability become a reality after the training is completed?

Many school administrators have not taught English learners using sheltered instruction techniques, and they have not had the opportunity to participate in the same professional development as their teachers. Therefore, becoming knowledgeable and possessing a thorough understanding of the SIOP® Model provides administrators with the information they need to lead the school forward. You might want to consider:

- joining teachers in SIOP® professional sessions not as an observer but as an active participant;
- observing a SIOP® class alongside a SIOP® Coach and after the lesson, discussing what you both observed, what evidence you saw of effective implementation of SIOP® components and features, and how the teacher might be coached for continued progress in implementing the model; and
- having a "SIOP® minute" at each faculty meeting for teachers to share successes with implementation.

Professional Learning Communities (PLC) and Staff Collaboration

Effective school restructuring requires willing teachers who are motivated to action and who are able to transform knowledge about change into reality (Hord, 1997). A popular initiative over the past decade, Professional Learning Communities, lends itself well to implementation of the SIOP® Model, as numerous SIOP® districts throughout the United States have discovered. While *collaboration* among teachers has been encouraged for some time, Professional Learning Communities go beyond the notion of "planning and working together" by focusing on several core principles. DuFour (2004) and colleagues (DuFour, DuFour, Eaker, & Many, 2006) describe the core principles or the "big ideas" as follows:

1. *Ensuring that students learn.* While most school mission statements promise that students will learn, within a PLC, the entire staff works to achieve the mission by determining and implementing school practices and characteristics that have been proven effective at helping students achieve at high levels. Together, administrators and teachers ask
   a. What do we want each student to learn?
   b. How will we know when each student has learned it?
   c. How will we respond when a student experiences difficulty in learning?

   The SIOP® Model, with validated, effective teaching practices for English learners, focuses teachers on these three questions, lesson by lesson. Within a PLC, staff members collaboratively determine in a timely manner which students are not making expected progress, in part by examining student work. They then provide these students with immediate support through a systematic plan that requires students to receive assistance until content standards are mastered (DuFour, 2004). With content and language objectives as part of the SIOP® Model, teachers are able to determine throughout a lesson whether students are making progress toward mastery of content concepts. PLCs enable teachers to work together to assist all struggling students, including English learners.

2. *A culture of collaboration.* In order to attain the goal of learning for all, teachers and administrators in a PLC create structures that promote collaboration. "The powerful collaboration that characterizes professional learning communities is a systematic process in which teachers work together to analyze and improve their classroom practice. Teachers work in teams, engaging in an ongoing cycle of questions that promote deep team learning. This process, in turn, leads to higher levels of student achievement" (DuFour, 2004, p. 9).

   When teachers and administrators use the SIOP® protocol as the focus of team planning, observations, conferences, and peer coaching, conversations revolve around effective teaching practices, including what works and how we know it works. To reach this level of collaboration, many SIOP® schools engage in study groups around the components discussed in each chapter of *Making Content Comprehensible for English Learners* (Echevarria, Vogt, & Short, 2008).

3. *A focus on results.* Professional Learning Communities evaluate the effectiveness of their work on the basis of results. All educators in a school are responsible for the success of all students. Each teacher participates in identifying levels of student performance, establishing goals, and periodically and systematically providing evidence of progress. This focus requires teachers and administrators to challenge traditional practice and examine prevailing assumptions. This also requires a school's staff to move away from thinking of improvement goals that relate to issues outside of the classroom and instead attend to those goals that focus on student learning. In essence, this is what the SIOP® Model is all about—improved student achievement for all students, including English learners.

Hord (1997) reports that schools that are restructured around Professional Learning Communities produce positive outcomes for both students and staff. The outcomes for staff include

- reduced teacher isolation;
- increased commitment to the mission and goals of the school;
- shared responsibility for the total development of all students;
- powerful learning that defines effective instruction and practice;
- enhanced understanding of curriculum and the role of the teacher;
- higher satisfaction and morale; and
- reduced absenteeism.

Data Collection with the SIOP® Model

In order to determine the impact of the SIOP® Model on the achievement of English learners, it is important to have a systematic approach to collecting and using data. If you completed the action plan described in Chapter 4 (and found in Appendix D), you will have already begun thinking about a formative evaluation.

Some schools, such as the K–3 Lela Alston School in the Isaac School District (Phoenix, Arizona), decided at the outset of SIOP® implementation in 2002 that they would undertake no other professional development initiative for several years. With such an investment and sustained focus, they wanted to know the effect of the SIOP® Model on student performance, so they planned for data collection and analysis. As described in Chapter 3, they collected data on Arizona state exams for math, reading, and writing at grade 3 and compared their own results over time (from 2002–2004) and to those of similar schools in the district. They also wanted to determine the longitudinal impact of the SIOP® Model for students who stayed at the school from kindergarten through grade 3. They found in 2004 that students who had remained at the school for all four years and had had three years of SIOP® instruction performed amazingly well on the state exams. Eighty-six percent of those students achieved the proficient or above-proficient level on the test, results that were far superior to those of comparable district schools. The considerable academic growth made by the English learners who had remained in the school for all four years, taught by the staff of SIOP®-trained teachers and paraprofessionals, was attributed to the SIOP® Model's implementation and the leadership at the school by the principal and SIOP® Coaches. (For detailed information about the Lela Alston School's implementation of the SIOP® Model, see Echevarria, Short, & Vogt, 2008).

Other schools and districts throughout the United States have taken varied approaches to data collection during SIOP® implementation, using a combination of informal and formal assessments (e.g., standardized tests). Many have assessed English proficiency using standardized measures in addition to academic growth. Some schools and/or districts have kept data from classroom observations using the SIOP® protocol, measuring improvement in teacher instruction on the thirty features with the scoring rubric. What we have seen repeatedly is that in those districts where SIOP® implementation has been successful, data collection and analysis that focused on the components of effective instruction and the progress of English learners were common.

Teacher Evaluation and the SIOP® Protocol

When the SIOP® Model was created and validated, it was never the intent that the protocol be used for teacher evaluation. It was originally designed for research purposes—to measure implementation of the features—and then expanded for use in coaching, supervising student teachers, and assisting administrators in knowing what to look for in lessons when observing classrooms that included English learners. However, over the years, some districts have decided to use the SIOP® protocol as an instrument for periodic teacher evaluation. We do not advocate this practice, especially when teachers are learning the model, because when the SIOP® becomes evaluative rather than constructive and supportive, teachers may hesitate to try new techniques and resist implementing the model. Nonetheless, once SIOP® Model professional development has occurred, several districts have revised their existing evaluation instrument to include SIOP® features; others have correlated their instrument to the SIOP® components and features.

Whatever your decision, it is important to clearly determine what the role of the protocol will be as you begin the implementation process. Several considerations should be explored first. A few are highlighted here:

Union contract. Before imposing any new "evaluation model," policy, or procedure, school leaders would be wise to consult with their teachers' union. Understanding the policy for changing evaluation procedures is crucial if the SIOP® protocol will be used as an instrument of instructional change. Some districts have negotiated district evaluation policies by removing the 0–4 rating rubric and using the protocol as a checklist of features to include in effective instruction for English learners, rather than as an instrument of evaluation (as we suggest in Appendix C).

Skill, experience, and competency levels of teachers. No matter what format or procedure is used for evaluation, in order to restructure a school for improved teaching and learning, a wise administrator will consider the skill, experience, and competency levels of his or her teachers. As administrators and researchers in the area of teacher evaluation become more knowledgeable about indices of effective teacher performance, those in charge of teacher evaluation are beginning to look beyond the traditional "clinical supervision" model (Hunter, 1976; Pajak, 2003; Glickman, Gordon, & Ross-Gordon, 2006; Vogt & Shearer, 2007). More and more districts are understanding that just as students' needs must be considered and differentiated instruction applied, teachers' developmental levels must also be assessed with appropriate techniques so that meaningful performance evaluation methods will promote not only teachers' development but their students' as well.

Glickman (2002) suggests examining three structures beyond teacher evaluation for promoting collaboration that fosters more effective teaching practices:

- Peer coaching
- Critical friends
- Classroom action research teams or study groups

Regardless of which methods are used with which teachers, the SIOP® Model can be used as a basic rubric against which teacher performance and instructional growth can be measured. However, a strength of the SIOP® Model as an instructional assessment tool lies in the administrator's ability to

1. plan a lesson alongside the teacher using the protocol;

2. discuss the various components before and after a lesson is delivered;

3. articulate what the scoring numbers mean and might look like if optimal implementation is achieved;

4. interpret the ratings once they have been recorded after observing a teacher; and

5. explain the ratings so that goals can be set for both the teacher's instruction and students' learning.

Whether the teacher is novice, experienced, or expert, the SIOP® protocol serves as a versatile and adaptable instrument for restructuring and improving the teaching and learning experiences for all involved. By incorporating the protocol as part of the observation process, including conferencing and goal-setting, teachers will not only be more accountable but also will have concrete and specific standards against which they can measure their own teaching and lesson planning progress.

Effective Differentiated Instruction

Differentiated instruction is another common initiative, and from our experience, it must be considered when administrators and teachers implement the SIOP® Model. However, while nearly every educator supports differentiated instruction in principle, in reality it is a difficult concept for many teachers to put into practice. Most educators rightly believe it involves multiple groups doing different things at the same time. This implies, to many teachers, more work, more grading, less control, and at its worst, chaos.

Collaborative projects benefit English learners' language and content learning.

However, the SIOP® Model is all about appropriate differentiated instruction, and once teachers have learned to implement (over time) the eight components and thirty features, they are, for the most part, practicing effective differentiated instruction. As a definition for differentiated instruction, we offer the following:

> Differentiated instruction describes the practice of grouping students for specific reading and content lessons and activities according to their needs and strengths, and then, as needed, regrouping students for focused lessons or mini-lessons that may occur prior to, during, or after a content lesson. It also refers to meeting the social, emotional, and psychological needs of students so they can develop independence, confidence, and the ability to work with others.

Note the second sentence in this definition. In the former "tracking days," there was little understanding that fixed ability groups (think Bluebirds, Robins, and Buzzards) would have long-lasting, deleterious effects on students' psyches as well as achievement (Oakes, 1985). Therefore, today's notions of differentiated instruction are much more related to a flexible rather than static construct.

Within the SIOP® Model, the goals of differentiated instruction include the following:

- To meet English learners' assessed academic needs;
- To build upon English learners' assessed academic and personal strengths;
- To develop English learners' academic and personal confidence;
- To provide opportunities to students for social interaction and collaboration in order to strengthen English proficiency.

Part of the problem that teachers (and administrators) have with creating effective and appropriate differentiated classrooms is that it may be difficult to picture what such a classroom looks like. The following comparison of typical non-differentiated and differentiated classrooms may be helpful to you and to your teachers (see the boxed feature on the opposite page).

As you learn about and review each of the eight components and thirty features of the SIOP® Model, revisit the characteristics of a differentiated classroom. Which of the specific SIOP® features match the characteristics listed in the boxed feature? If you do this task, you will see that the characteristics of a differentiated classroom are a close match with the features of the SIOP® Model. As teachers learn how to implement the model, they are also learning how to provide effective differentiated instruction.

Sustaining the SIOP® Model Over Time

All of us who have been educators for many years realize how challenging it can be to sustain reform efforts. That is one reason why this chapter has focused on restructuring schools and systemic change. SIOP® Model implementation must be for the long haul if English learners' academic achievement and language development are priorities.

A Comparison of Non-Differentiated and Differentiated Classrooms

In Non-Differentiated Classrooms . . .	**In Differentiated Classrooms . . .**
• The teacher is the one who knows the objectives for the lesson.	• Both the teacher and students know clearly the content and language objectives for each lesson.
• Student differences and interests are not particularly relevant during lesson planning.	• Student differences, interests, and needs guide lesson planning.
• Assessment is used to see "who got it," and it occurs at the end of a lesson or unit. The same assessment is used for all students with a single standard for grading.	• Assessment is ongoing, continuous, and includes multiple indicators, products, and ways of responding. The grading standard may be adjusted based on student proficiencies, including English.
• Whole-class teaching prevails. The "cemetery model" is the predominant classroom organizational structure (all desks in a row).	• Grouping of students for instruction is frequent and flexible. Desks and tables are grouped for most activities and instruction.
• Instructional goals focus on content coverage (based on standards).	• Instructional goals focus on individual students' mastery of content and language objectives (derived from standards).
• Assignments, texts, and tasks are the same for all students.	• A variety of texts, tasks, and options is evident.
• The daily schedule and time allotments are relatively inflexible.	• Time is allocated flexibly based on student attainment of objectives.
• A search for one correct answer and/or single interpretation is the norm.	• Multiple perspectives are routinely sought.
• The preponderance of talk is the teacher's.	• Talk is shared between students and teacher.
• Teacher-directed questioning is common with the IRE pattern dominating (question initiation, student response, teacher evaluation).	• Structured discussion is carefully planned and facilitated.
• High-level thinking questions and tasks are reserved for the highest-achieving students.	• High-level thinking questions and tasks are the norm for all students.
	• Students know and follow classroom routines.
	• All students are believed capable of achieving learning goals and standards.

Therefore, as part of the SIOP® implementation process, thought must be given to sustainability so that the following well-known phenomenon does not occur:

> In this all-too familiar cycle, initial enthusiasm gives way to confusion about the fundamental concepts driving the initiative, followed by inevitable implementation problems, the conclusion that the reform has failed to bring about the desired results, abandonment of the reform, and the launch of a new search for the next promising

initiative. Another reform movement has come and gone, reinforcing the conventional education wisdom that promises, "This too shall pass" (DuFour, 2004, p. 6).

Throughout this chapter, we have discussed ways to promote sustainability of the SIOP® Model, including the involvement of informed, committed principals who know the model well. In addition, we recommend the following:

1. **Create a plan for new and transfer teachers.** In the districts that have successfully implemented the model, SIOP® training is ongoing so that new and transfer teachers have the opportunity to participate in professional development. For example, when Lisa Roberts was an elementary school principal from the Boise School District, she was selected to open a new school, and as a requirement for transferring to the school, all teacher applicants had to agree in writing to take part in professional development on the SIOP® Model. She made it clear to everyone that this new school was a "SIOP® School." In other districts, SIOP® Coaches work with new and transfer teachers to ensure their knowledge and implementation of the model.

2. **Create a plan for change in district personnel.** A few districts have implemented the SIOP® Model across all schools with the full and enthusiastic support of the superintendent, only to have him or her transfer to another district. The new superintendent arrives with different ideas and initiatives and doesn't know about the SIOP® Model, and implementation takes a backseat to his or her other priorities. Have a plan in place that includes other knowledgeable district administrative personnel, so as new people are interviewed and hired, the SIOP® Model is explained as an instructional focus for the district. Also, don't forget the school board. In successful SIOP® schools and districts, school board members have also received an overview of the SIOP® Model and regular updates as to the progress of English learners in the district.

3. **Create a plan for the development of new sheltered classes.** This is especially important at the high school level, where one academic course (such as Biology) is followed by another in a sequence (such as Chemistry). If English learners are enrolled in a sheltered Biology course, there needs to be a sheltered Chemistry class for them to move to the following semester or year. For example, Boise School District began SIOP® implementation with professional development on the SIOP® Model for teachers of high school English learners in the Language Academy, which is designed for newcomer students who have been in the country for less than two years. Subsequent SIOP® training was designed for those who would be teaching sheltered content classes for students coming out of the Language Academy. As new sheltered courses were added, additional teachers were trained in the model. It is important to note that all teachers in the district had a one-day overview of the SIOP® Model early in the course of implementation.

   It is also important to design high school sheltered courses to comply with state standards and curriculum guidelines so core credit for graduation may be granted to ELs who pass the courses. The Charlotte-Mecklenburg school district has electronically linked SIOP® content course numbers to the state course numbers to facilitate the process.

4. **Keep the conversations going once SIOP® professional development is completed.** If you have Professional Learning Communities within your school, discussion and sharing among teachers is routine. If you don't have collaborative

structures in place, encourage and facilitate the sharing of ideas, frank discussion of challenges, and celebration of successes related to the SIOP® Model. Lisa Roberts, the former Boise elementary school principal, devoted time at each staff meeting for a SIOP® teacher to share successful instructional techniques for English learners. Teachers volunteered for this informative and engaging part of the meeting.

5. **Involve parents and families.** This recommendation is sometimes challenging when parents of English learners lack English proficiency, and therefore, may feel unprepared to become involved in school activities. Claremore Public Schools in Claremore, Oklahoma, faced this challenge by issuing invitations to an open house in multiple languages for the ELs' parents. The invitations were not only sent home with students but were posted where parents would see them—in neighborhood grocery stores, the library, gas stations, and the laundromat. The open house ultimately involved many parents of ELs who had not attended any school activities before. The point here is that when parents of English learners are welcomed and become involved because the school has made an effort to include them, they are unlikely to let a reform effort that focuses on the effective and appropriate instruction for their children lapse. They become an important and integral part of the SIOP® team.

Key Points Summary

- In order for any school or district restructuring effort to be successful, planning for its implementation, including the professional development of all instructional staff and stakeholders, is essential.

- When educators understand that the SIOP® Model is not a "program," or "fad," or "latest-greatest thing in education," comprehensive implementation of its components and features is far more likely.

- When educators, administrators, teachers, and support staff are encouraged to collaborate and share successes and challenges, the SIOP® Model has a better chance for success.

- The English learners in our schools deserve our best efforts to educate them in an equitable, effective, and appropriate manner through differentiated instruction, and under the tutelage of informed, committed, knowledgeable teachers and administrators.

Reflect and Apply

1. As you look back over this chapter, what do you suspect will be the greatest challenge an administrator will face in sustaining SIOP® Model implementation?

2. Reflect on other initiatives and/or reform efforts currently being advocated in your district:
   a. What are the instructional goals of these initiatives?
   b. How do they correlate with the instructional goals of the SIOP® Model?
   c. Where are the similarities and differences, and do any of them relate to the education of English learners?

chapter 6

Implementing the SIOP® Model: Frequently Asked Questions

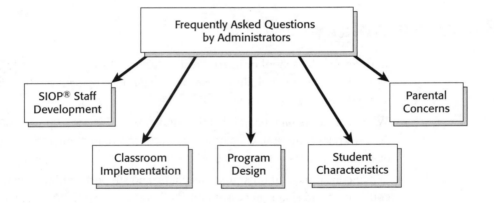

The SIOP® Model is a phenomenal program of acceleration and should be viewed as such. School administrators, school counselors, and teachers should present it in this way rather than as a program of remediation. I believe doing this will help address parental concerns. We all learn many things from each other in a classroom. Strong teachers will find this easy to do. Additionally, it's important to remember that many ELLs are working at or above grade level—SIOP® courses are not just for lower-level students—either in language development needs or content-area needs.

Joan Rolston, ESL Program Counselor, Charlotte-Mecklenburg Schools,
North Carolina

In our work with teachers and administrators all over the United States, we are frequently asked questions about the implementation of the SIOP® Model in schools and districts. In this chapter we address the most frequent and relevant questions based upon our experiences and those of SIOP® implementers. We have organized the questions into the following categories: SIOP® staff development, classroom implementation of the SIOP® Model, program design, student characteristics, and parental concerns. A resource for a broader range of English learner programmatic and instructional issues is *English Language Learners at School* (Hamayan & Freeman, 2006).

SIOP® Staff Development

How do I select teachers for SIOP® Model staff development?

As an administrator, you have several options for selecting teachers who will participate in SIOP® professional development. Your selection process should consider the following:

- Long-term goal (e.g., Will this be a multiyear initiative that aims to train all teachers schoolwide in the SIOP® Model?)
- Needs of the students (e.g., Are they experiencing a lack of success in some key courses that could change if the teachers had more support in working with ELs?)
- Data on student performance (e.g., Are there particular subjects or grade levels where students on the whole are not achieving?)
- Resources (e.g., How much time and funding is available for SIOP® staff development?)

One rule of thumb is to begin with teachers who volunteer to participate. By analyzing the course schedules designed for English learners, you may select those courses that are most critical (e.g., those needed for high school graduation) and seek volunteers from that pool of teachers. In this way, the courses will be taught by those who know how to integrate language and content learning. In an elementary school, you may want one volunteer at each grade level trained first so as students move up the grades, there will be an appropriate placement for them. In secondary schools, you might ask for volunteers from teachers of sheltered content courses.

We strongly recommend that ESL and language specialists be included in the SIOP® professional development sessions with the content teachers. Creating opportunities for collaboration will lead to better implementation—content teachers will recognize colleagues who can act as resources for language objectives and language development techniques, and language teachers will see content teachers as sources for the content objectives, subject-specific vocabulary, and background knowledge they need to incorporate in their content-based ESL classes. Certainly, special educators and reading specialists should be involved as well.

Should I train the whole staff in the SIOP® Model?

Schools such as Lela Alston Elementary School (described in Chapter 3) have had significant success in raising student test scores after schoolwide SIOP® training and implementation. Other schools have seen similar progress (see *Implementing the SIOP® Model through Effective Professional Development and Coaching*, Echevarria, Short, & Vogt, 2008, for details) when the whole staff has been trained. These results indicate the value of schoolwide training. However, the decision needs to be site-specific. If your school has a large population of English learners (15 to 20 percent or more, for instance), it is worth planning to train the whole staff. Even if all the teachers do not have English learners who are in the ESL or bilingual program, they are likely to have some students who have exited such programs. Given the research on student achievement discussed in Chapter 1, we know that many of these exited (or monitored) students are still on the path to full academic literacy and would be more successful in classes with teachers trained to make content comprehensible while furthering their language skills.

Some administrators have asked about the "specials" or "electives" teachers. Although the elective classes may not be as academically rigorous as, say, physics or fifth-grade mathematics, the teachers play important roles in helping students with social language and in developing some of their special talents. Some of the elective classes, like health, require a large amount of reading, so developing the students' literacy skills is key in that class. Others, like keyboarding, may be a course that ELs are always scheduled into because it is assumed the course doesn't require a lot of language. Nonetheless, with a trained SIOP® keyboarding teacher, a great deal of English language development can take place in such courses as students not only learn to type, but type their own texts, search the Internet and read posted information, participate in Web Quests, and so forth.

How can we help resistant and/or reluctant teachers?

As districts implement the SIOP® Model, they often encounter some reluctant or resistant teachers. Just as there is a need to differentiate for students, it is also important to do so for teachers. Acknowledging that change is a process and teachers may be at different stages within this process can help teachers, administrators, and staff developers identify the reasons for the resistance. Toll (2005, pp. 41–2) points out that 10 to 20 percent of a school's staff are likely to be teachers who "put on the brakes." Some of these are teachers who resist change in principle or who believe a new initiative is a fad that they can wait out. Others in the group may feel unprepared to take on the new initiative and do it well.

The following ideas have been helpful in our experience:

- Principals initially invite key teachers to be trained in the SIOP® Model. These selected teachers demonstrate openness to incorporating the SIOP® Model and are interested in refining their classroom instruction. It is helpful to have a few teachers who are viewed as leaders by their colleagues in the group.

- Principals or other administrators support the teachers during the training as well as in the implementation stages. Teachers who view their administrator as someone who will follow through at the building level, giving support with the implementation process, are more receptive to the training.

- Successes are celebrated and made visible. SIOP® teachers who are experiencing success with the English learners should be acknowledged by the administration, perhaps in a faculty meeting or through a hallway bulletin board display of student work. A SIOP® Teacher of the Month award could be established. In addition, some of the enthusiastic SIOP® teachers might open their rooms to peer observations.

- Follow-up support after the initial training has helped many teachers overcome their initial reluctance. Helping teachers problem-solve specific areas of the SIOP® Model at the classroom and building level has assisted teachers in implementation. What was perceived as resistance often changes as teachers begin to see success for their students and themselves.

- Administrators and teachers can jointly examine student performance data. Some teachers believe they are doing a good job and do not have to change their instructional practice. Look for evidence to prove or disprove this theory. If the ELs in these resistant teachers' classes are performing well on formal assessments and other measures, then maybe the teachers do not need the staff development. However, if the students are not performing well, then the teachers should join the staff development program.

How many days should we spend on staff development?

The answer to this question depends in part on the time available for professional development and the speed desired for teachers to learn the model. It is important to plan not only staff development days that introduce teachers to the SIOP® components but also follow-up workshops to deepen their knowledge and give them a chance to share successes and challenges with the implementation process.

We have learned several things over the years that we have supported SIOP® staff development. The professional development should be ongoing and at best, job embedded. Specifically, spread workshops and other training opportunities throughout the year. Allow the teachers to learn about the SIOP® Model and try it out, perhaps focusing on one component at a time. Then they can discuss how the SIOP® lessons have gone and learn some more. Many districts prefer to introduce the SIOP® Model in a cumulative fashion, building knowledge of the components and practice with the features over time. Needless to say, avoid the five-day summer workshop if there are no follow-up workshops during the year. The teachers require direct support to implement SIOP® lessons successfully and need a chance to debrief on what they are learning and get coaching on what they still need to learn.

Many of the districts and schools devote the equivalent of six to eight days to help teachers learn the model well. Lela Alston Elementary School spent two years training the teachers, one full staff development day per quarter, plus after-school meetings and coaching sessions. In Clifton Public Schools (New Jersey), each cohort of teachers had seven workshop days scheduled in the first year of training—a three-day summer institute and four follow-up days, approximately one per quarter. The second year included three additional days—one before school began and one each semester. These follow-up days in the second year focused on unit lesson planning.

Classroom Implementation of the SIOP® Model

How do we ensure the SIOP® Model is implemented in the classroom?

Leadership and support are critical elements in ensuring that SIOP® implementation takes place. As a school administrator, it is important to convey clearly and frequently that you value SIOP® teaching and expect to observe it in classrooms. When meeting with teachers, stopping in their classrooms, and chatting after school, be sure to ask about the SIOP® implementation. Share your expectations for posted objectives on the board, activities that promote student interaction on content-related topics, use of supplementary materials, and so on.

When teachers begin using SIOP® Model instruction, they need support. A recommendation is to arrange for a SIOP® Coach who can help with lesson planning, visit classes, and provide feedback. If a coach is not possible at this time, work toward having one the following year. Find ways for teachers to partner or form small SIOP® groups so they can support one another. If you "buy a sub for a day," you can offer the teachers a chance to observe one another. With one substitute teacher, six to eight teachers could visit another teacher's classroom in one day. The sub would cover a different teacher's class each period (or hour in an elementary school).

Joan Rolston, the ESL program counselor in Charlotte-Mecklenburg (North Carolina) Schools offers the following sage advice:

> The important thing is for the entire school faculty and staff to see the big picture. We can no longer allow English language learners to be an ancillary population of students. The SIOP® Model reinforces the idea that all educators are language teachers—and this helps *every* student—including our English-only students. Remember, success feels good and is motivating—from both the students' side and the teachers' side.

How can teachers write lesson plans that incorporate the SIOP® components?

Teachers may want to begin with an existing lesson plan and determine which features of the SIOP® Model are already present. They can then identify those features that must be included (e.g., language objectives) or need more emphasis (e.g., explicitly teaching learning strategies or choosing appropriate cooperative grouping structures). Working with a partner or coach, they can revise, or SIOPize, the original lesson plan.

Although some teachers may be disinclined to write out SIOP® lessons at first, we urge them to do so as a means for internalizing the model and for focusing on the language and content objectives to ensure they are addressed throughout the lesson. Instead of overwhelming an elementary school teacher responsible for all core subjects or a secondary school teacher with five different course preparations by asking them to write lessons for each subject or class, we suggest they select one subject or one class period to start. In our experience, the act of writing out lessons helps teachers learn the model better. An added benefit is that the best SIOP® practices permeate the other subjects and course periods rather naturally even if teachers don't write out detailed plans for those courses.

Another approach is the cumulative one. Some sites introduce one component of the SIOP® Model at a time; for example, September focuses on Lesson Preparation, October on Building Background, and so forth. Teachers are asked to write lessons that incorporate the components studied to date. So in September they concentrate on the Lesson Preparation features; by December they may be focusing on the features from Preparation, Building Background, Comprehensible Input, and Strategies.

In *Making Content Comprehensible for English Learners: The SIOP® Model* (Echevarria, Vogt, & Short, 2008), four SIOP® lesson planning templates are provided. Teachers may select one of these formats to develop their own lessons, or create one based on school or district guidelines. An advantage to using a SIOP® lesson plan format is that it reinforces the essential elements of sheltered instruction. Sample lesson plans that can serve as models may also be found in Chapters 5 and 6 of the *Making Content Comprehensible* book, in Chapter 7 of the *Implementing the SIOP Model* book (Echevarria, Short, & Vogt, 2008), throughout the *99 Ideas and Activities* book (Vogt & Echevarria, 2008), and on the SIOP® Institute (www.SIOPinstitute.net) and the Center for Applied Linguistics' (www.cal.org) Web sites.

Does a teacher have to incorporate all thirty SIOP® features in every lesson? If not, which must be observed in every lesson?

Although we do not expect all thirty features to be present in every lesson, most will be once teachers have internalized the SIOP® Model. It is worth noting that we do not define a lesson as one class period; rather we define it according to the objectives set for that particular lesson, which may stretch over several class periods. Within this explanation, the expectation would be to observe most of the features in any given period and all thirty presented over the course of a week. At all times, we expect to see content and language objectives posted and activities and tasks that support the posted objectives. In *Making Content Comprehensible for English Learners* (Echevarria, Vogt, & Short, 2008), we explain that five of the features may not be present at some point during a lesson. These are

- adaptation of content (this might not be needed if content and materials suit the students' proficiency levels);
- concepts explicitly linked to linking to students' background (may not be needed later in a unit or with a review lesson);
- ample opportunities for students to clarify concepts in L1 (concepts may be comprehensible in English);
- hands-on materials or manipulatives to practice using new content knowledge (the lesson may not yet be at a stage for practice or may be beyond); and
- activities provided to apply content and language knowledge (the lesson may not yet be at a stage for application).

If a lesson continues over several days, it is still valuable for the teacher to wrap up each day with a review of the key vocabulary and concepts and to continue the next day with a review of the lesson objectives.

When teachers initially begin writing their lessons following the SIOP® Model, they may find that they already incorporate many of the features, but some others may need more emphasis. The most common area targeted for special emphasis is identifying and constructing appropriate language objectives. This feature, which is vital for ELs, is often the most difficult for content teachers who do not have a background in second language acquisition or ESL methodology. Staff developers and coaches should provide plenty of practice and support in setting language objectives aligned to the subject area and in determining appropriate tasks and activities for students to undertake.

How can I support SIOP® coaching?

If you have a say in the selection process, choose your SIOP® Coach or coaches carefully. Do not just add another item to the job description of a current literacy coach or teacher resource specialist. Be sure the coach knows the SIOP® Model deeply, understands second language learners and the challenges they face in mainstream classrooms, and also knows how to mentor teachers. Skillful coaches acknowledge the unique needs of adult learners. Some districts have chosen stellar classroom teachers to become their staff developers; however, these teachers may have little or no experience in working with adult learners (or resistant teachers) and so need additional training. Teachers are more receptive to coaches they see as competent in their field and who understand the day-to-day requirements of teaching.

Once the coach has been selected, the administrator needs to offer unqualified support of his or her task. This is done by scheduling time for coaching, providing meeting space for the coaches to meet one-on-one with teachers or in small groups, having reasonable expectations about how many teachers a coach can successfully coach, and making sure the coach has the professional development tools and materials he or she needs to ensure that teachers implement the SIOP® Model to a high degree. Also don't forget that the SIOP® Coach needs opportunities for professional development as well.

How soon should I expect teachers to implement the SIOP® Model well in their lessons?

How soon teachers will implement the SIOP® Model well will vary by individual. The answer depends on the teachers' background and experience with ESL methods, second language acquisition, and sheltered instruction. As we find with our students, some teachers will adapt to SIOP® Model instruction rapidly, some will make steady progress, and some will move at a slower pace. Our research on the SIOP® Model in Clifton (New Jersey) Public Schools (Center for Applied Linguistics, 2007) showed that teachers need one to two years to implement the model consistently to a high degree. That research did show, however, that if teachers learning the model had coaching and also were part of an existing SIOP® team, their teaching transformation took place more rapidly.

Should I use the SIOP® protocol when observing and evaluating teachers?

We recommend that school administrators use the SIOP® protocol in a checklist format when observing the lessons of new SIOP® teachers. Appendix C is the SIOP® protocol modified into a checklist where an observer can record the level of implementation of the SIOP® features. An observer can note if the feature was Highly Evident, Somewhat Evident, or Not Evident in a lesson. We do not recommend the protocol as a teacher evaluation tool, particularly while teachers are learning the model.

If the eight components are being taught and implemented over time, then only the components already taught should be on the checklist. However, as new components are added, the checklist can grow until it represents the complete protocol.

Program Design

Can the SIOP® Model be used in any program type?

Absolutely. The SIOP® Model can be used and has been used effectively in a wide range of program types. It is appropriate any time that students are learning content through a new language. The SIOP® Model suits programs with an English language focus, such as ESL, sheltered, and structured English immersion programs. It is also valuable in bilingual programs, such as transitional and developmental bilingual, dual language, and two-way immersion programs. When bilingual programs begin the transition process for students, by providing some courses in English, the SIOP® Model is an excellent way to strengthen the learners' academic literacy. One participant on the SIOP® Institute's Listserv, Jill, offered this perspective: "SIOP® is a guide for us to develop solid lessons, modifications, and extensions for our students. SIOP® is a tool that we use to ensure that our students are active participants in their own learning."

The SIOP® Model has also been used in special education programs. The emphasis on language development, hands-on practice, and teacher modeling makes it an effective approach for students with disabilities. In our original SIOP® research study, students who were identified as having disabilities made significant academic progress when teachers used the SIOP® Model.

Do I need to set up special SIOP® courses in the master schedule?

Although not required, it is recommended that some sheltered (or SIOP®) courses be developed and added to the master schedule. Administrators are a very important part of this scheduling process, as are the guidance counselors. Joan Rolston of Charlotte-Mecklenburg Schools advises principals, "Being flexible with a master schedule is vital. Master schedules may change from year to year. Be prepared to look at what is working and where improvements can be made." Counselors can help with scheduling the students and should know which teachers have been trained in the SIOP® Model and which have not. Unfortunately, we have heard repeatedly that in some schools ELs are placed into a course simply because it has fewer students, not because the teacher has the skills and knowledge to instruct the ELs effectively.

In planning the master schedule, it is not only the course designations for ELs that are important but also the teachers' schedules. SIOP® teachers need to have opportunities to collaborate with colleagues on lesson design and other aspects of implementation. Setting aside common planning time among members of a SIOP® cohort should be a goal.

Most of the sites that have designated sheltered content courses have been careful to design the curricula to match the state standards and have assigned qualified content teachers to them. This careful planning is particularly critical at the high school level, because in this way, state departments of education have approved these courses as bearing core credits for high school graduation.[1]

---

[1]In some states, students need to pass end-of-course tests as well as pass the course in order to receive the core credit.

What do you do when there are few English learners in your school or district?

National demographic data projects that most teachers will have an EL or former EL student in their class, if not at present then in the near future. As discussed in Chapter 1, a growing number of ELs are enrolled in smaller, non-urban school districts. Ideally, all mainstream teachers would have special preparation and training in sheltered instruction to accommodate these students, but at the time of this writing only four states make any such professional preparation a requirement for initial teacher state certification. That is one reason why the SIOP® Model has been widely used for inservice staff development.

If a good proportion of teachers are trained in the SIOP® Model in a school, it makes it easier to accommodate the second language learners. We need to include these students in grade-level content courses and also provide targeted language development classes so they gain proficiency in academic English. In schools where there are few English learners, students can be grouped or clustered in selected classrooms or on teams with teachers who have had SIOP® Model training. It is helpful, therefore, to think about the series of courses ELs will take from year to year and make sure that at each successive grade level, key teachers are able to implement the SIOP® Model. The SIOP® teachers can employ specific strategies to differentiate instruction according to the needs of all the students in the class, but in particular, they make the grade-level content comprehensible so English learners can participate in the regular classroom activities.

Student Characteristics

What about using the SIOP® Model in mixed classrooms, those with English learners and native English speakers?

The SIOP® Model offers value in circumstances like this where native English speakers and ELs study together. Because the model addresses grade-level curricula and standards, both student groups have their needs met. Furthermore, the attention to academic literacy that the SIOP® Model calls for is often beneficial to many native English speakers as well.

One of the SIOP® National Faculty members, Liz Warner, has described how she addresses this question:

> One of the first things I might explain is that the SIOP® Model asks teachers to differentiate within their lessons according to language proficiency and ability of the students *without* compromising the academic/cognitive demand. We are not changing the curriculum, the scope and sequence, or the academic vocabulary and rigor because we are held responsible for teaching grade-level standards for the grade level we teach. We are simply saying that by sheltering our lessons and teaching, we can make the content, rigor, and the like, more accessible when language is a barrier. The SIOP® Model allows for differentiation, which might not happen in a whole group/one-size-fits-all lesson.

What do we do about newcomer students?

Newcomer students also benefit from SIOP® Model instruction. They need differentiated lessons that truly integrate language learning and content instruction. However, it is important to remember that the SIOP® Model is an instructional approach; it is not a newcomer program. The placement of newcomer students into SIOP® classes is best within the context of designated newcomer courses. Knowing the educational backgrounds and needs of these students is critical. Charlotte-Mecklenburg counselors are expected to spend time with these students during the intake process in order to place them appropriately, because a lack of English skills does not necessarily mean the students lack grade-level content knowledge.

It is certainly possible that some newcomer ELs may not be ready for grade-level concepts if they have interrupted educational backgrounds. For instance, a thirteen-year-old who has had only two years of schooling is unlikely to be prepared for Pre-Algebra. The curricula of some SIOP® classes for newcomers with interrupted education and low literacy may therefore need to be adapted. The best scenario in this case would be establishing new courses that accelerate the students' learning so they can catch up to their grade-level peers.

We have many students who exhibit learning difficulties, but we don't know if it is because they need to learn English or if there is an actual learning disability. How can we determine if these students should be referred for special education?

Learning through a new language is very challenging. Some of the behaviors manifested by ELs may resemble students with learning disabilities or language disorders, such as passive participation and problems comprehending text. When a learning problem is suspected, the first step is to examine the learning environment. Does the teacher provide instruction that is comprehensible and scaffolded to accommodate the student's language proficiency? Is sufficient modeling and practice provided? Does the student differ significantly from others who have similar backgrounds (i.e., language, culture, country of origin, socioeconomic level)? Does the family believe the student has language or learning difficulties? Do similar difficulties manifest themselves in the student's first language?

Once some background has been gathered about the student, academic interventions should be tried and documented. Through a Response to Intervention approach, the first level of intervention is to change instruction to ensure that the student experiences success and makes progress. We believe that high-quality SIOP® instruction will help to overcome many of the obstacles that prevent ELs from achieving. If the student doesn't respond positively to the changes, other interventions should be tried, such as more small-group instruction or specific skill instruction.

The most important consideration to keep in mind is that ELs typically have not had the kinds of background experiences that academic texts and tasks presume students have. Many learning problems can be attributed to this lack of background knowledge, limited vocabulary in English, and low levels of English proficiency. Since only about 5 to 10 percent of any population will have specific learning disabilities, academic difficulties are usually attributable to instructional practices that don't meet the needs of English learners. Appropriate instruction is often exactly what struggling students need to reach higher levels of academic achievement. Research on the SIOP® Model has shown its effectiveness for students with learning disabilities, making it an excellent, research-based instructional model to use with these learners.

How can we tell if a student has a reading problem or lacks proficiency for reading text in English?

This is a serious problem because of the difficulty in adequately assessing reading ability for students acquiring English (see Chapter 10 in Echevarria, Vogt, & Short, 2008, for a detailed discussion of assessment problems with ELs' reading abilities). In essence, most traditional reading assessments (of phonemic awareness, phonics, vocabulary, fluency, and comprehension) do not result in reliable findings for English learners. For Spanish speakers, increasing numbers of assessments are available, but the field is woefully lacking in comprehensive reading assessments in other languages that will provide insights into ELs' reading abilities. If your students speak languages other than English, enlist the help of adults in the community who are literate in students' native languages (L1), and try to obtain some L1 reading materials. Asking students (especially those who are in the upper grades) to read the L1 materials may be helpful in assessing native language literacy. Also, contact the students' parents to inquire about the child's literacy development and schooling experiences. In other words, use all resources at your disposal to try to determine a student's L1 literacy ability. Abundant research indicates that a student's L1 literacy skill has a direct impact on his or her second language literacy development.

Parental Concerns

How do you respond to parent concerns that their average or accelerated students will be short-changed with attention to the needs of English learners?

In every classroom, school, and district across the country, regardless of content or grade level, teachers face the same challenge: how do I instruct such a diverse group of learners? These children enter the school doors with different background experiences, educational histories, requisite skills, learning styles, talents, and motivations. The idea that "one" instructional approach or methodology can be successful with all learners is a myth.

With the current reform movements of the past fifteen years, public schools must account for all students reaching content-specific standards. Therefore, teachers are required to use different instructional strategies and techniques to ensure that all students are learning the prescribed content at the appropriate rate.

The unit and lesson design of the SIOP® Model is based on content, grade-level objectives, and language objectives for second language learners. These are explicitly written in lesson plans and displayed in the classroom for students to see. Although these language objectives are vital for English learners, we have noted that other students profit from their inclusion in the lesson. In fact, because SIOP® teachers are encouraged to build in more interaction, more practice and application, native English speakers have reported that they enjoy those classes more. One teacher in the research study in New Jersey found that the students in the class where she used the SIOP® Model did better on the tests than the students in her other classes did, and so she expanded her use of this type of instruction to all her classes.

The reality of public education in the United States today is of classrooms with diverse learners who must meet state and national educational accountability measures. The SIOP® Model provides a framework for meeting these specific educational requirements for all learners. Erick, a participant on the SIOP® Institute Listserv, expressed it succinctly: "Teach to the highest, scaffold for the lowest."

How do you respond to bilingual parents' concerns regarding appropriate instruction for their children?

Effective sheltered instruction (that is, the SIOP® Model) is an integral component of any comprehensive bilingual program. Any time teachers are providing academic instruction to students who are not fully proficient in the language of instruction (whether that language is English or another language), the teacher must employ strategies for making the content comprehensible and provide opportunities for interaction. These are precisely the elements addressed in the SIOP® Model. The goal of any comprehensive bilingual program is that students become bilingual and biliterate. Skilled bilingual teachers must shelter the content to reach this goal. The longer-term programs such as developmental bilingual and dual-language education increase the amount of instructional time students spend in English-medium subject-area classes as students progress up the grades. The SIOP® Model is an excellent framework for those classes.

appendix a: Program Alternatives for English Learners

	Sheltered Instruction in English	Newcomer Programs	Transitional Bilingual	Developmental Bilingual	Two-way Immersion
Language Goals	Academic English proficiency	English proficiency	Transition to all-English instruction	Bilingualism	Bilingualism
Cultural Goals	Understanding of and integration into mainstream American culture	Understanding of and integration into mainstream American culture	Understanding of and integration into mainstream American culture	Integration into mainstream American culture and maintenance of home/heritage culture	Maintenance/integration into mainstream American culture and appreciation of other culture
Academic Goals	Same as district/program goals for all students	Varied	Same as district/program goals for all students	Same as district/program goals for all students	Same as district/program goals for all students
Student Characteristics	Limited or no English; Some programs mix native and nonnative English speakers	Limited or no English Low-level literacy Recent arrival Variety of language/cultural backgrounds	Limited or no English All students have same L1 Variety of cultural backgrounds	Limited or no English All students have same L1 Variety of cultural backgrounds	Native English speakers and students with limited or no English Variety of cultural backgrounds
Grades Served	All grades (during transition to English)	K–12; most prevalent at middle/high school levels	Primary and elementary grades, few secondary	Elementary grades	K–5, K–8, or K–12
Entry Grades	Any grade	Most students enter in middle or high school	K, 1, 2 usually	K, 1, 2	K, 1 usually
Length of Student Participation	Varied: 1–3 years or as needed	Usually 1–3 semesters	2–4 years	Usually 6 years (+K), preferably 12 years (+K)	Usually 6 years (+K), preferably 12 years (+K)
Participation of Mainstream Teachers	Yes; preferable if mainstream teachers have SI training	Yes; mainstream teachers must have training in SI	Yes; mainstream teachers must have training in SI	No; stand-alone program with its own specially trained teachers	Yes; mainstream teachers with special training
Teacher Qualifications	Often certified ESL or bilingual teachers and content teachers with SI training Preferably bilingual	Regular certification Training in SI Preferably bilingual	Bilingual certificate	Bilingual-multicultural certificate Bilingual proficiency	Bilingual/immersion certification Bilingual proficiency Multicultural training
Instructional Materials, Texts, Visual Aids	In English with adaptations; visuals; realia; culturally appropriate	In L1 or in English with adaptations	In L1 and English; English materials adapted to students' proficiency levels	In L1 and English; English materials adapted to students' proficiency levels	In minority language and English, as required by curriculum of study

Adapted from Genesee, F. (Ed.). (1999). *Program Alternatives for Linguistically Diverse Students*. Educational Practice Report No. 1. Santa Cruz, CA & Washington, DC: Center for Research on Education, Diversity & Excellence. Used with permission.

appendix b: The Sheltered Instruction Observation Protocol (SIOP®)

Observer(s): _____

Date: _____

Grade: _____

ESL Level: _____

Teacher: _____

School: _____

Class/Topic: _____

Lesson: Multiday   Single-day   (*circle one*)

Total Points Possible: 120 (Subtract 4 points for each NA given: _____)

Total Points Earned: _____   Percentage Score: _____

Directions: Circle the number that best reflects what you observe in a sheltered lesson. You may give a score from 0–4 (or NA on selected items). Cite under "Comments" specific examples of the behaviors observed.

LESSON PREPARATION

4	3	2	1	0
1. **Content objectives** clearly defined, displayed, and reviewed with students		**Content objectives** for students implied		No clearly defined **content objectives** for students

Comments:

4	3	2	1	0
2. **Language objectives** clearly defined, displayed, and reviewed with students		**Language objectives** for students implied		No clearly defined **language objectives** for students

Comments:

4	3	2	1	0
3. **Content concepts** appropriate for age and educational background level of students		**Content concepts** somewhat appropriate for age and educational background level of students		**Content concepts** inappropriate for age and educational background level of students

Comments:

4	3	2	1	0
4. **Supplementary materials** used to a high degree, making the lesson clear and meaningful (e.g., computer programs, graphs, models, visuals)		Some use of **supplementary materials**		No use of **supplementary materials**

Comments:

(Echevarria, Vogt, & Short, 2000; 2004; 2008)

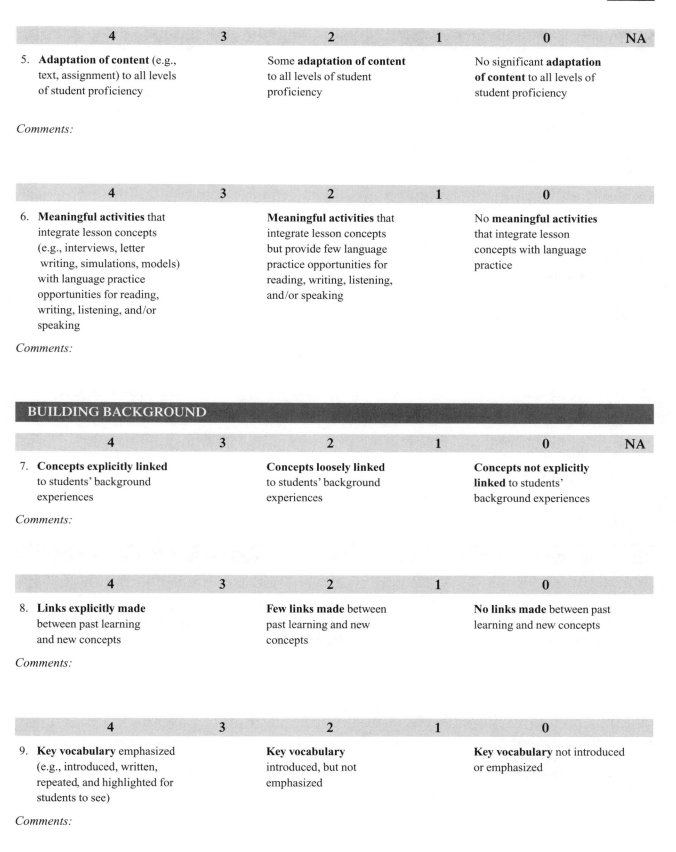

4	3	2	1	0	NA

5. **Adaptation of content** (e.g., text, assignment) to all levels of student proficiency

Some **adaptation of content** to all levels of student proficiency

No significant **adaptation of content** to all levels of student proficiency

Comments:

4	3	2	1	0

6. **Meaningful activities** that integrate lesson concepts (e.g., interviews, letter writing, simulations, models) with language practice opportunities for reading, writing, listening, and/or speaking

Meaningful activities that integrate lesson concepts but provide few language practice opportunities for reading, writing, listening, and/or speaking

No **meaningful activities** that integrate lesson concepts with language practice

Comments:

BUILDING BACKGROUND

4	3	2	1	0	NA

7. **Concepts explicitly linked** to students' background experiences

Concepts loosely linked to students' background experiences

Concepts not explicitly linked to students' background experiences

Comments:

4	3	2	1	0

8. **Links explicitly made** between past learning and new concepts

Few links made between past learning and new concepts

No links made between past learning and new concepts

Comments:

4	3	2	1	0

9. **Key vocabulary** emphasized (e.g., introduced, written, repeated, and highlighted for students to see)

Key vocabulary introduced, but not emphasized

Key vocabulary not introduced or emphasized

Comments:

COMPREHENSIBLE INPUT

4	3	2	1	0
10. **Speech** appropriate for students' proficiency levels (e.g., slower rate, enunciation, and simple sentence structure for beginners)		**Speech** sometimes inappropriate for students' proficiency levels		**Speech** inappropriate for students' proficiency levels

Comments:

4	3	2	1	0
11. **Clear explanation** of academic tasks		**Unclear** explanation of academic tasks		**No** explanation of academic tasks

Comments:

4	3	2	1	0
12. **A variety of techniques** used to make content concepts clear (e.g., modeling, visuals, hands-on activities, demonstrations, gestures, body language)		Some **techniques** used to make content concepts clear		No **techniques** used to make concepts clear

Comments:

STRATEGIES

4	3	2	1	0
13. Ample opportunities provided for students to use **learning strategies**		Inadequate opportunities provided for students to use **learning strategies**		No opportunity provided for students to use **learning strategies**

Comments:

4	3	2	1	0
14. **Scaffolding techniques** consistently used, assisting and supporting student understanding (e.g., think-alouds)		**Scaffolding techniques** occasionally used		**Scaffolding techniques** not used

Comments:

4	3	2	1	0

15. A variety of **questions or tasks that promote higher-order thinking skills** (e.g., literal, analytical, and interpretive questions)

Infrequent **questions or tasks that promote higher-order thinking skills**

No **questions or tasks that promote higher-order thinking skills**

Comments:

INTERACTION

4	3	2	1	0

16. Frequent opportunities for **interaction** and discussion between teacher/student and among students, which encourage elaborated responses about lesson concepts

Interaction mostly teacher-dominated with some opportunities for students to talk about or question lesson concepts

Interaction teacher-dominated with no opportunities for students to discuss lesson concepts

Comments:

4	3	2	1	0

17. **Grouping configurations** support language and content objectives of the lesson

Grouping configurations unevenly support the language and content objectives

Grouping configurations do not support the language and content objectives

Comments:

4	3	2	1	0

18. Sufficient **wait time for student responses** consistently provided

Sufficient **wait time for student responses** occasionally provided

Sufficient **wait time for student responses** not provided

Comments:

4	3	2	1	0	NA

19. Ample opportunities for students to **clarify key concepts in L1** as needed with aide, peer, or L1 text

Some opportunities for students to **clarify key concepts in L1**

No opportunities for students to **clarify key concepts in L1**

Comments:

PRACTICE AND APPLICATION

4	3	2	1	0	NA

20. **Hands-on materials and/or manipulatives** provided for students to practice using new content knowledge

Few **hands-on materials and/or manipulatives** provided for students to practice using new content knowledge

No **hands-on materials and/or manipulatives** provided for students to practice using new content knowledge

Comments:

4	3	2	1	0	NA

21. Activities provided for students to **apply content and language knowledge** in the classroom

Activities provided for students to **apply** either **content or language knowledge** in the classroom

No activities provided for students to **apply content and language knowledge** in the classroom

Comments:

4	3	2	1	0

22. Activities integrate all **language skills** (i.e., reading, writing, listening, and speaking)

Activities integrate some **language skills**

Activities do not integrate **language skills**

Comments:

LESSON DELIVERY

4	3	2	1	0

23. **Content objectives** clearly supported by lesson delivery

Content objectives somewhat supported by lesson delivery

Content objectives not supported by lesson delivery

Comments:

4	3	2	1	0

24. **Language objectives** clearly supported by lesson delivery

Language objectives somewhat supported by lesson delivery

Language objectives not supported by lesson delivery

Comments:

4	3	2	1	0

25. **Students engaged** approximately 90% to 100% of the period

Students engaged approximately 70% of the period

Students engaged less than 50% of the period

Comments:

4	3	2	1	0

26. **Pacing** of the lesson appropriate to students' ability levels

Pacing generally appropriate, but at times too fast or too slow

Pacing inappropriate to students' ability levels

Comments:

REVIEW AND ASSESSMENT

4	3	2	1	0

27. Comprehensive **review of key vocabulary**

Uneven **review of key vocabulary**

No **review of key vocabulary**

Comments:

4	3	2	1	0

28. Comprehensive **review of key content concepts**

Uneven **review of key content concepts**

No **review of key content concepts**

Comments:

4	3	2	1	0

29. Regular **feedback** provided to students on their output (e.g., language, content, work)

Inconsistent **feedback** provided to students on their output

No **feedback** provided to students on their output

Comments:

4	3	2	1	0

30. **Assessment of student comprehension and learning** of all lesson objectives (e.g., spot checking, group response) throughout the lesson

Assessment of student comprehension and learning of some lesson objectives

No **assessment of student comprehension and learning** of lesson objectives

Comments:

The Sheltered Instruction Observation Protocol (SIOP®)

(Echevarria, Vogt, & Short, 2000; 2004; 2008)

Observer(s): _____ Teacher: _____

Date: _____ School: _____

Grade: _____ Class/Topic: _____

ESL Level: _____ Lesson: Multiday Single-day *(circle one)*

Total Points Possible: 120 (Subtract 4 points for each NA given) _____

Total Points Earned: _____ Percentage Score: _____

Directions: Circle the number that best reflects what you observe in a sheltered lesson. You may give a score from 0–4 (or NA on selected items). Cite under "Comments" specific examples of the behaviors observed.

	Highly Evident		Somewhat Evident		Not Evident	
Lesson Preparation	**4**	**3**	**2**	**1**	**0**	
1. **Content objectives** clearly defined, displayed, and reviewed with students	❑	❑	❑	❑	❑	
2. **Language objectives** clearly defined, displayed, and reviewed with students	❑	❑	❑	❑	❑	
3. **Content concepts** appropriate for age and educational background level of students	❑	❑	❑	❑	❑	
4. **Supplementary materials** used to a high degree, making the lesson clear and meaningful (e.g., computer programs, graphs, models, visuals)	❑	❑	❑	❑	❑	**NA**
5. **Adaptation of content** (e.g., text, assignment) to all levels of student proficiency	❑	❑	❑	❑	❑	❑
6. **Meaningful activities** that integrate lesson concepts (e.g., surveys, letter writing, simulations, constructing models) with language practice opportunities for reading, writing, listening, and/or speaking	❑	❑	❑	❑	❑	

Comments:

	4	**3**	**2**	**1**	**0**	**NA**
Building Background						
7. **Concepts explicitly linked** to students' background experiences	❑	❑	❑	❑	❑	❑
8. **Links explicitly made** between past learning and new concepts	❑	❑	❑	❑	❑	
9. **Key vocabulary** emphasized (e.g., introduced, written, repeated, and highlighted for students to see)	❑	❑	❑	❑	❑	

Comments:

	4	**3**	**2**	**1**	**0**
Comprehensible Input					
10. **Speech** appropriate for students' proficiency level (e.g., slower rate, enunciation, and simple sentence structure for beginners)	❑	❑	❑	❑	❑
11. **Clear explanation** of academic tasks	❑	❑	❑	❑	❑
12. **A variety of techniques** used to make content concepts clear (e.g., modeling, visuals, hands-on activities, demonstrations, gestures, body language)	❑	❑	❑	❑	❑

Comments:

	4	**3**	**2**	**1**	**0**
Strategies					
13. Ample opportunities provided for students to use **learning strategies**	❑	❑	❑	❑	❑

	Highly Evident		Somewhat Evident		Not Evident	
	4	**3**	**2**	**1**	**0**	
14. **Scaffolding techniques** consistently used assisting and supporting student understanding (e.g., think-alouds)	❑	❑	❑	❑	❑	
15. A variety of **questions or tasks that promote higher-order thinking skills** (e.g., literal, analytical, and interpretive questions) *Comments:*	❑	❑	❑	❑	❑	

Interaction	**4**	**3**	**2**	**1**	**0**	
16. Frequent opportunities for **interaction** and discussion between teacher/student and among students, which encourage elaborated responses about lesson concepts	❑	❑	❑	❑	❑	
17. **Grouping configurations** support language and content objectives of the lesson	❑	❑	❑	❑	❑	
18. Sufficient **wait time for student responses** consistently provided	❑	❑	❑	❑	❑	**NA**
19. Ample opportunities for students to **clarify key concepts in L1** as needed with aide, peer, or L1 text *Comments:*	❑	❑	❑	❑	❑	❑

Practice and Application	**4**	**3**	**2**	**1**	**0**	**NA**
20. **Hands-on materials and/or manipulatives** provided for students to practice using new content knowledge	❑	❑	❑	❑	❑	❑
21. Activities provided for students to **apply content and language knowledge** in the classroom	❑	❑	❑	❑	❑	**NA** ❑
22. Activities integrate all **language skills** (i.e., reading, writing, listening, and speaking) *Comments:*	❑	❑	❑	❑	❑	

Lesson Delivery	**4**	**3**	**2**	**1**	**0**	
23. **Content objectives** clearly supported by lesson delivery	❑	❑	❑	❑	❑	
24. **Language objectives** clearly supported by lesson delivery	❑	❑	❑	❑	❑	
25. **Students engaged** approximately 90% to 100% of the period	❑	❑	❑	❑	❑	
26. **Pacing** of the lesson appropriate to students' ability level *Comments:*	❑	❑	❑	❑	❑	

Review and Assessment	**4**	**3**	**2**	**1**	**0**	
27. Comprehensive **review of key vocabulary**	❑	❑	❑	❑	❑	
28. Comprehensive **review of key content concepts**	❑	❑	❑	❑	❑	
29. Regular **feedback** provided to students on their output (e.g., language, content, work)	❑	❑	❑	❑	❑	
30. **Assessment of student comprehension and learning** of all lesson objectives (e.g., spot checking, group response) throughout the lesson *Comments:*	❑	❑	❑	❑	❑	

appendix c: The SIOP® Checklist

The Sheltered Instruction
Observation Protocol (SIOP®)
(Echevarria, Vogt, & Short, 2008)

Observer(s): _____
Date: _____
Grade: _____
ESL Level: _____

Teacher: _____
School: _____
Class/Topic: _____
Lesson: Multiday Single-day *(circle one)*

	Highly Evident	Somewhat Evident	Not Evident

Preparation

1. <u>Content objectives</u> clearly defined, displayed, and reviewed with students

2. <u>Language objectives</u> clearly defined, displayed, and reviewed with students

3. <u>Content concepts</u> appropriate for age and educational background level of students

4. <u>Supplementary materials</u> used to a high degree, making the lesson clear and meaningful (computer programs, graphs, visuals)

5. <u>Adaptation of content</u> (e.g., text, assignment) to all levels of student proficiency

6. <u>Meaningful activities</u> that integrate lesson concepts (e.g., interviews, letter writing, simulations, models) with language practice opportunities for reading, writing, listening, and/or speaking

Comments:

Building Background

7. <u>Concepts explicitly linked</u> to students' background experiences
8. <u>Links explicitly made</u> between past learning and new concepts
9. <u>Key vocabulary</u> emphasized (e.g., introduced, written, repeated, and highlighted for students to see)

Comments:

Comprehensible Input

10. <u>Speech</u> appropriate for students' proficiency levels (e.g., slower rate, enunciation, and simple sentence structure for beginners)
11. <u>Clear explanation</u> of academic tasks
12. <u>A variety of techniques</u> used to make content concepts clear (e.g., modeling visuals, hands-on activities, demonstrations, gestures, body language)

Comments:

	Highly Evident	Somewhat Evident	Not Evident

Strategies

13. Ample opportunities provided for students to use <u>learning strategies</u>

14. <u>Scaffolding techniques</u> consistently used, assisting and supporting student understanding (e.g., think-alouds)

15. A variety of <u>questions or tasks that promote higher-order thinking skills</u> (e.g., literal, analytical, and interpretive questions)

Comments:

Interaction

16. Frequent opportunities for <u>interaction</u> and discussion between teacher/student and among students, which encourage elaborated responses about lesson concepts

17. <u>Grouping configurations</u> support language and content objectives of the lesson

18. Sufficient <u>wait time for student responses</u> consistently provided

19. Ample opportunities for students <u>to clarify key concepts in L1</u>

Comments:

Practice/Application

20. <u>Hands-on materials and/or manipulatives</u> provided for students to practice using new content knowledge

21. Activities provided for students to <u>apply content and language knowledge</u> in the classroom

22. Activities integrate all <u>language skills</u> (i.e., reading, writing, listening, and speaking)

Comments:

Lesson Delivery

23. <u>Content objectives</u> clearly supported by lesson delivery

24. <u>Language objectives</u> clearly supported by lesson delivery

25. <u>Students engaged</u> approximately 90% to 100% of the period

26. <u>Pacing</u> of the lesson appropriate to the students' ability level

Comments:

Review/Assessment

27. Comprehensive <u>review of key vocabulary</u>

28. Comprehensive <u>review of key content concepts</u>

29. Regular <u>feedback</u> provided to students on their output (e.g., language, content, work)

30. <u>Assessment of student comprehension and learning</u> of all lesson objectives (e.g., spot checking, group response) throughout the lesson

Comments:

Examine the Academic Performance of English Learners

How are the English learners doing in different subject areas? At different grade levels, schools, or school levels (e.g., elementary, middle, or high)? What may be the areas to target?

Set a Goal for SIOP® Model Implementation

What is the overall goal for this initiative?

What you would like to have happen in the short term (e.g., one year)?

Over the long term (e.g., several years)?

How will you measure progress toward meeting the goal?

Establish Responsibilities

Who will lead SIOP® implementation? Who will assist? What will be each person's responsibility (e.g., point person, coach, fiscal manager)?

Plan SIOP® Staff Development

Who will conduct the staff development? What topics will be covered in initial SIOP® workshops?

Will you have follow-up meetings to continue learning about the SIOP® Model and discussing classroom practice? If so, list possible workshop topics.

Who will lead the follow-up activities?

What type of accountability will be in place (e.g., submit SIOP® lesson plans, be observed, observe and rate peers)?

Who will be in the first cohort of teachers learning the SIOP® Model?

· a p p e n d i x ●

103

What is the time frame for the first cohort?

Who will be in future cohorts and when will they participate?

Besides teachers, which other staff will receive SIOP® professional development and what will it entail?

Additional Supports for Teachers

What additional supports are needed to help teachers use the SIOP® Model in class (e.g., supplementary resources, curriculum materials, master schedule adjustments)?

Create a Preliminary SIOP® Coaching Plan

Who is a potential SIOP® Coach? What training will the coach need before getting started?

What resources and time can the coach be given to support classroom implementation?

Secure Funding

What funds are available for SIOP® Model implementation?

How can they be earmarked to sustain implementation over time?

Consider Planning a Formative Evaluation

Who can work on this effort?

Which data will be collected and analyzed for teachers and students? What might be a data collection schedule?

Create a Realistic Timeline

Look over all the plans. How and when can these SIOP® Implementation efforts be enacted? Create a timeline and organize by staff, activity, and funding source.

glossary

Academic language: Language used in formal contexts for academic subjects. The aspect of language connected with literacy and academic achievement. This includes technical and academic terms (*see* Cognitive/Academic Language Proficiency—CALP).

Assessment: The orderly process of gathering, analyzing, interpreting, and reporting student performance, ideally from multiple sources over a period of time.

Basic Interpersonal Communicative Skills (BICS): Face-to-face conversational fluency, including mastery of pronunciation, vocabulary, and grammar. English language learners typically acquire conversational language used in everyday activities before they develop more complex, conceptual language proficiency.

Bilingual instruction: School instruction using two languages, generally a native language of the student and a second language. The amount of time that each language is used depends on the type of bilingual program, its specific objectives, and students' level of language proficiency.

Cognitive Academic Language Proficiency (CALP): Language proficiency associated with schooling, and the abstract language abilities required for academic work. A more complex, conceptual, linguistic ability that includes analysis, synthesis, and evaluation.

Cognitive coaching: A process used by an instructional coach as a means for understanding an observed teacher's thoughts and actions while planning and delivering lessons and for encouraging teacher reflection. Cognitive coaching generally involves a planning conference (pre-observation), the observation, and a reflective conference (post-observation). Cognitive coaching should be nonevaluative, but should guide teachers professionally.

Content-based ESL: An instructional approach in which content topics are used as the vehicle for second language learning. A system of instruction in which teachers use a variety of instructional techniques as a way of developing second language, content, cognitive, and study skills, often delivered through thematic units.

Content objectives: Statements that identify what students should know and be able to do in particular content areas. They support school district and state content standards and learning outcomes, and they guide teaching and learning in the classroom.

Content standards: Definitions of what students are expected to know and be capable of doing for a given content area; the knowledge and skills that need to be taught in order for students to reach competency; what students are expected to learn and what schools are expected to teach. May be national, state, or local-level standards.

Culture: The customs, lifestyle, traditions, behavior, attitudes, and artifacts of a given people. Culture also encompasses the ways people organize and interpret the world, and the way events are perceived based on established social norms. A system of standards for understanding the world.

Dialect: The form of a language peculiar to a specific region. Features a variation in vocabulary, grammar, and pronunciation.

Differentiated instruction: The practice of grouping students for specific lessons (e.g., reading, math) and assigning activities according to their needs and strengths. Students may be regrouped for focused lessons or mini-lessons that may occur prior to, during, or after a content lesson. A goal is to meet the social, emotional, and psychological needs of students so they can develop independence, confidence, and the ability to work with others.

Engagement: When students are fully taking part in a lesson, they are said to be engaged. This is a holistic term that encompasses listening, reading, writing, responding, and discussing. The level of students' engagement during a lesson may be assessed to a greater or lesser degree. A low SIOP® score for engagement would imply frequent chatting, daydreaming, nonattention, and other off-task behaviors.

English learners (ELs): Children and adults who are learning English as a second or additional language. This term may apply to learners across various levels of proficiency in English. ELs may also be referred to as English language learners (ELLs), non–English speaking (NES), limited English proficient (LEP), and a non-native speaker (NNS).

ESL: English as a second language. Used to refer to programs and classes to teach students English as a second (additional) language.

ESOL: English speakers of other languages. Students whose first language is not English and who do not write, speak, and understand the language as well as their classmates. May also refer to a program for these students.

Evaluation: Judgments about students' learning made by interpreting and analyzing assessment data; the process of judging achievement, growth, product, processes, or changes in these; judgments of education programs. The processes of assessment and evaluation can be viewed as progressive: first, assessment; then, evaluation.

Formative evaluation: Ongoing collection, analysis, and reporting of information about student performance for purposes of instruction and learning.

Grouping: The assignment of students into groups or classes for instruction, such as by age, ability, or achievement; or within classes, such as by reading ability, proficiency, language background, or interests.

Home language: The language, or languages, spoken in the student's home by people who live there. Also referred to as first language (L1), primary language, or native language.

Informal assessment: Appraisal of student performance through unstructured observation; characterized as frequent, ongoing, continuous, and involving simple but important techniques such as verbal checks for understanding, teacher-created assessments, and other nonstandardized procedures. This type of assessment provides teachers with immediate feedback.

Inter-rater reliability: Measures of the degree of agreement between two different raters on separate ratings of one assessment indicator using the same scale and criteria.

L1: First language. A widely used abbreviation for the primary, home, or native language.

Language minority: In the United States, a student whose primary language is not English. The individual students' ability to speak English will vary.

Language objectives: Statements that identify what students should know and be able to do while using English (or another language). They support students' language development, often focusing on vocabulary, functional language, reading, and writing skills, and so forth.

Language proficiency: An individual's competence in using a language for basic communication and for academic purposes. May be categorized as stages of language acquisition (*see* Stages of language proficiency).

Limited English Proficient (LEP): A term used to refer to a student with restricted understanding or use of written and spoken English; a learner who is still developing competence in using English. The federal government uses the term LEP while EL or ELL is more commonly used in schools.

Multilingualism: The ability to speak more than two languages; proficiency in more than two languages.

Native English speaker: An individual whose first language is English.

Native language: An individual's first, primary, or home language (L1).

Non–English speaking (NES): Individuals who are in an English-speaking environment (such as U.S. schools) but who have not acquired any English proficiency.

Nonverbal communication: Paralinguistic messages such as intonation, stress, pauses and rate of speech, and nonlinguistic messages such as gestures, facial expressions, and body language that can accompany speech or be conveyed without the aid of speech.

Performance assessment: A measure of educational achievement where students produce a response, create a product, or apply knowledge in ways similar to tasks required in the instructional environment. The performance measures are analyzed and interpreted according to preset criteria.

Portfolio assessment: A type of performance assessment that involves gathering multiple indicators of student progress to support course goals in a dynamic, ongoing process. Portfolios are purposeful collections of student performance that evince students' efforts, progress, and achievement over time.

Primary language: An individual's first, home, or native language (L1).

Professional Learning Community (PLC): A reform structure in schools whereby a collaborative group of experienced educators (teachers and administrators) work toward a common goal, usually of improved student achievement. PLCs often examine student data, support instructional initiatives, conduct peer observations, and share a vision and commitment to student learning.

Pull-out instruction: Students are "pulled-out" from their regular classes for special classes of ESL instruction, remediation, or acceleration.

Realia: Real-life objects and artifacts used to supplement teaching; can provide effective visual scaffolds for English learners.

Reliability: Statistical consistency in measurements and tests, such as the extent to which two assessments measure student performance in the same way.

Rubrics: Statements that describe indicators of performance, which include scoring criteria, on a continuum; may be described as "developmental" (e.g., emergent, beginning, developing, proficient) or "evaluative" (e.g., exceptional, thorough, adequate, inadequate).

Scaffolding: Adult (e.g., teacher) support for learning and student performance of the tasks through instruction, modeling, questioning, feedback, graphic organizers, and more, across successive engagements. These supports are gradually withdrawn, thus transferring more and more autonomy to the child. Scaffolding activities provide support for learning that can be removed as learners are able to demonstrate strategic behaviors in their own learning activities.

SDAIE (Specially Designed Academic Instruction in English): A term for sheltered instruction used mostly in California. It features strategies and techniques for making content understandable for English learners. Although some SDAIE techniques are research based, SDAIE itself has not been scientifically validated. (*See* Sheltered instruction.)

Self-contained ESL class: A class consisting solely of English speakers of other languages for the purpose of learning English; content may also be taught. An effective alternative to pull-out instruction.

Sheltered instruction (SI): A means for making content comprehensible for English learners while they are developing English proficiency. The SIOP® is a validated model of sheltered instruction. Sheltered classrooms, which may, in a mix of native English speakers and English learners or only ELs, integrate language and content while infusing sociocultural awareness. (*See* SDAIE and SIOP®.)

SIOP® (Sheltered Instruction Observation Protocol): A scientifically validated model of sheltered instruction designed to make grade-level academic content understandable for English learners while at the same time developing their English language. The protocol and lesson planning guide ensure that teachers are consistently implementing practices known to be effective for English learners.

Social language: Basic language proficiency associated with fluency in day-to-day situations, including the classroom (*see* Basic Interpersonal Communicative Skills—BICS).

Stages of language proficiency: Students learning language progress through stages. The stages are labeled differently across geographic regions. The following are from Krashen and Terrell. (1983, 1984)

Preproduction: Students at this stage are not ready to produce much language, so they primarily communicate with gestures and actions. They are absorbing the new language and developing receptive vocabulary.

Early production: Students at this level speak using one or two words or short phrases. Their receptive vocabulary is developing; they understand approximately one thousand words. Students can answer "who, what, and where" questions with limited expression.

Speech emergence: Students speak in longer phrases and complete sentences. However, they may experience frustration at not being able to express completely what they know. Although the number of errors they make increases, they can communicate ideas and the quantity of speech they produce increases.

Intermediate fluency: Students may appear to be fluent; they engage in conversation and produce connected narrative. Errors are usually of style or usage. Lessons continue to expand receptive vocabulary, and activities develop higher levels of language use in content areas. Students at this level are able to communicate effectively.

Advanced fluency: Students communicate very effectively, orally and in writing, in social and academic settings.

Standard American English: "That variety of American English in which most educational texts, government, and media publications are written in the United States; English as it is spoken and written by those groups with social, economic, and political power in the United States. Standard American English is a relative concept, varying widely in pronunciation and in idiomatic use but maintaining a fairly uniform grammatical structure" (Harris & Hodges, 1995, p. 241).

Standards-based assessment: Assessment involving the planning, gathering, analyzing, and reporting of a student's performance according to the ESL and/or district content standards.

Strategies: Mental processes and plans that people use to help them comprehend, learn, and retain new information. There are three types of strategies—cognitive, metacognitive, and social/affective—and these are consciously adapted and monitored during reading, writing, and learning.

Summative evaluation: The final collection, analysis, and reporting of information about student achievement or program effectiveness at the end of a given time frame.

Task: An activity that calls for a response to a question, issue, or problem.

Validity: A statistical measure of an assessment's match between the information collected and its stated purpose; evidence that inferences from evaluation are trustworthy.

references

August, D., & Shanahan, T. (Eds.). (2006). *Developing literacy in second-language learners: A report of the National Literacy Panel on Language-Minority Children and Youth.* Mahwah, NJ: Erlbaum.

Baker, C. (1992). *Attitudes and language.* Clevedon, England: Multilingual Matters.

Bambino, D. (March 2002). Redesigning professional development: Critical friends. *Educational Leadership, 59* (6), 25–27.

Batalova, J., Fix, M., & Murray, J. (2005). *English language learner adolescents: Demographics and literacy achievements.* Report to the Center for Applied Linguistics. Washington, DC: Migration Policy Institute.

Bauder, T. (2007). Setting the stage for SIOP coaching. In Sherris, A., Bauder, T., & Hillyard, L., *An insider's guide to SIOP coaching* (pp. 15–25). Washington, DC: Center for Applied Linguistics.

Beck, I.L., Perfetti, C., & McKeown, M.G. (1982). Effects of long-term vocabulary instruction on lexical access and reading comprehension. *Journal of Educational Psychology, 74*, 506–521.

Biancarosa, G., & Snow, C. (2004). *Reading next: A vision for action and research in middle and high school literacy.* Report to the Carnegie Corporation of New York. Washington, DC: Alliance for Excellent Education.

Biemiller, A. (2001). Teaching vocabulary: Early, direct and sequential. *American Educator*, Spring.

Brown, H.D. (2000). *Principles of language learning and teaching.* White Plains, NY: Pearson Education.

California Department of Education, Educational Demographics Unit. (2004). *Statewide Stanford 9 test results for reading: Number of students tested and percent scoring at or above the 50th percentile ranking (NPR).* Retrieved February 23, 2004, from www.cde.ca.gov/dataquest.

Capps, R., Fix, M., Murray, J., Ost, J., Passel, J.S., & Herwantoro, S. (2005). *The new demography of America's schools: Immigration and the No Child Left Behind Act.* Washington, DC: Urban Institute.

Carlo, M.S., August, D., McLaughlin, B., Snow, C. E., Dressler, C., Lippman, D., Lively, T., & White, C.

(2004). Closing the gap: Addressing the vocabulary needs of English language learners in bilingual and mainstream classrooms. *Reading Research Quarterly, 39*(2), 188–215.

Center for Applied Linguistics. (2007). *Academic literacy through sheltered instruction for secondary English language learners.* Final Report to the Carnegie Corporation of New York. Washington, DC: Center for Applied Linguistics.

Collier, V. (1987). Age and rate of acquisition of second language for academic purposes. *TESOL Quarterly 21*(3), 617–641.

Costa, A.L., & Garmston, R.J. (2002). *Cognitive coaching: A foundation for renaissance schools.* 2nd ed. Norwood, MA: Christopher-Gordon.

Crawford, J. (2003). Communicative approaches to second-language acquisition: The bridge to second-language literacy. In G. Garcia (Ed.), *English learners: Reaching the highest levels of English literacy.* Newark, DE: International Reading Association.

Cushman, K. (May 1998). *How friends can be critical as schools make essential changes.* Oxon Hill, MD: Coalition of Essential Schools.

Cummins, J. (1984). *Bilingualism and special education: Issues in assessment and pedagogy.* Clevedon, England: Multilingual Matters.

Cummins, J. (2000). *Language, power and pedagogy.* Clevedon, England: Multilingual Matters.

Cummins, J. (2006). How long does it take for an English language learner to become proficient in a second language? In E. Hamayan & R. Freeman (Eds.), *English language learners at school: A guide for administrators* (pp. 59–61). Philadelphia: Caslon Publishing.

Darling-Hammond, L. (1998). *Teacher learning that supports student learning. Educational Leadership, 55*(5), 6–11.

DuFour, R. (2004). What is a "Professional Learning Community?" *Educational Leadership, 61*(8), 6–11.

DuFour, R., DuFour, R., Eaker, R., & Many, T. (2006). *Learning by doing: A handbook for Professional Learning Communities at work.* Bloomington, IN: Solution Tree.

Echevarria, J., & Graves, A. (2007). *Sheltered content instruction: Teaching English learners with diverse abilities.* 3ʳᵈ ed. Boston: Allyn & Bacon.

Echevarria, J., Short, D., & Powers, K. (2006). School reform and standards-based education: An instructional model for English language learners. *Journal of Educational Research, 99*(4), 195–211.

Echevarria, J., Short, D., & Vogt, ME. (2008). *Implementing the SIOP® model through effective professional development and coaching.* Boston, MA: Pearson/Allyn & Bacon.

Echevarria, J., Vogt, M.E., & Short, D. (2000). *Making content comprehensible for English language learners: The SIOP® model.* Needham Heights, MA: Allyn & Bacon.

Echevarria, J., Vogt, M.E., & Short, D. (2004). *Making content comprehensible for English learners: The SIOP® model.* 2ⁿᵈ Ed. Boston: Pearson/Allyn & Bacon.

Echevarria, J., Vogt, M.E., & Short, D. (2008). *Making content comprehensible for English learners: The SIOP® model.* 3ʳᵈ Ed. Boston: Pearson/Allyn & Bacon.

Edley, C., Jr., & Wald, J. (2002, December 16). The grade retention fallacy. *The Boston Globe.*

Fillmore, L.W., & C. Snow. (2002). What teachers need to know about language. In C. T. Adger, C. E. Snow & D. Christian (Eds.), *What teachers need to know about language* (pp. 7–53). McHenry, IL: Delta Systems and Center for Applied Linguistics.

Garcia, G., & Beltran, D. (2003). Revisioning the blueprint: Building for the academic success of English learners. In G. Garcia (Ed.), *English learners: Reaching the highest levels of English literacy.* Newark, DE: International Reading Association.

Garcia, G.E., & Godina, H. (2004). Addressing the literacy needs of adolescent English language learners. In T. Jetton & J. Dole (Eds.), *Adolescent literacy: Research and practice* (pp. 304–320). New York: The Guildford Press.

Garet, M.S., Porter, A.C., Desimone, L., Binnan, B.F., & Yoon, K.S. (2001). What makes professional development effective? Results from a national sample of teachers. *American Educational Research Journal, 38*, 915–945.

Genesee, F. (Ed.). (1999). *Program alternatives for linguistically diverse students.* Educational Practice Report No. 1. Santa Cruz and Washington, DC: Center for Research on Education, Diversity & Excellence.

Genesee, F., Geva, E., Dressler, C., & Kamil, M. (2006). Synthesis: Cross-linguistic relationships. In D. August & T. Shanahan (Eds.), *Developing literacy in second-language learners.* Mahwah, NJ: Lawrence Erlbaum Associates.

Genesee, F., Lindholm-Leary, K., Saunders, W., & Christian, D. (2006). *Educating English language learners: A synthesis of research evidence.* New York: Cambridge University Press.

Gersten, R., S. Brengelman, et al. (1994). Effective instruction for culturally and linguistically diverse students: A reconceptualization. *Focus on Exceptional Children, 27*, 1–16.

Glick, J.E., & White, M.J. (2004). Post-secondary school participation of immigrant and native youth: The role of familial resources and educational expectations. *Social Science Research, 33*, 272–299.

Glickman, C. (2002). *Leadership for learning.* Alexandria, VA: Association for Supervision and Curriculum Development.

Glickman, C.D., Gordon, S.P., & Ross-Gordon, J. M. (2006). *SuperVision and instructional leadership: A developmental approach.* 7ᵗʰ Ed. Boston: Pearson Allyn & Bacon.

Goldenberg, C. (2004). *Successful school change: Creating settings to improve teaching and learning.* New York: Columbia University Press.

Goldenberg, C., Rueda, R., & August, D. (2006). Sociocultural influences on the literacy attainment of language-minority children and youth. In D. August & T. Shanahan (Eds.), *Developing literacy in second-language learners* (pp. 269–318). Mahwah, NJ: Lawrence Erlbaum Associates.

Graham, S., & Perin, D. (2007). *Writing next: Effective strategies to improve writing of adolescents in middle and high schools.* A report to the Carnegie Corporation of New York. Washington, DC: Alliance for Excellent Education.

Graves, M. (2006). *The vocabulary book: Learning & instruction.* New York: Teachers College Press.

Grigg, W., Daane, M., Jin, Y., & Campbell, J. (2003). *The nation's report card: Reading 2002.* Washington, DC: U.S. Department of Education.

Guarino, A.J., Echevarria, J., Short, D., Schick, J.E., Forbes, S., & Rueda, R. (2001). The Sheltered Instruction Observation Protocol. *Journal of Research in Education, 11*(1), 138–140.

Hamayan, E., & Freeman, R. (Eds.) (2006). *English language learners at school: A guide for administrators*. Philadelphia: Caslon Publishing.

Hoffman, L., & Sable, J.(2006). *Public elementary and secondary students, staff, schools, and school districts: School year 2003–2004*. Washington, DC: National Center for Educational Statistics.

Hord, S.M. (1997). *Professional learning communities: Communities of continuous inquiry and improvement*. Austin, TX: Southwest Educational Development Laboratory.

Hunter, M. (1976). *Improved instruction*. El Segundo, CA.

Kamil, M. (2003). *Adolescents and literacy: Reading for the 21ˢᵗ century*. Washington, DC: Alliance for Excellent Education.

Kindler, A. (2002). *Survey of the states' limited English proficient students and available educational programs and services. 2000–01 summary report*. Washington, DC: National Clearinghouse for English Language Acquisition.

Klein, S., Bugarin, R., Beltranena, R., & McArthur, E. (2004). *Language minorities and their educational and labor market indicators—Recent trends*. (NCES 2004–009). Washington, DC: U.S. Department of Education, National Center for Educational Statistics.

Kober, N., Zabala, D., Chudowsky, N., Chudowsky, V., Gayler, K., & McMurrer, J. (2006). *State high school exit exams: A challenging year*. Washington, DC: Center for Education Policy.

Krashen, S. (1982). Accounting for child-adult differences in second language rate and attainment. In S. Krashen, R. Scarcella, & M. Long (Eds.), *Child-adult differences in second language acquisition*. Rowley, MA: Newbury House.

Lambert, L. (1998). *Building leadership capacity in schools*. Alexandria, VA: Association for Supervision and Curriculum Development.

Lemke, J. (1988). Genres, semantics, and classroom education. *Linguistics and Education 1*, 81–99.

Lesaux, N., Koda, K., Siegel, L., & Shanahan, T. (2006). Development of literacy. In D. August, & Shanahan, T. (Eds.), *Developing literacy in second-language learners* (pp. 75–122). Mahwah, NJ: Lawrence Erlbaum Associates.

Lewis, C. (2002). *Lesson study: A handbook for teacher-led instructional change*. Philadelphia: Research for Better Schools.

Lipson, M., & Wixson, K. (2007). *Assessment & instruction of reading and writing disability*. 3rd ed. New York: Longman.

Long, M. (2007). *Problems in SLA*. Mahwah, NJ: Lawrence Erlbaum Associates.

Nagy, W. (1997). On the role of context in first- and second-language vocabulary learning. In N. Schmitt & M. McCarthy (Eds.), *Vocabulary: Description, acquisition and pedagogy* (pp. 64–83). Cambridge: Cambridge University Press.

Nagy, W.E., & Scott, J.A. (2000). Vocabulary processes. In R. Barr, M.L. Kamil, P. Mosenthal, & P.D. Pearson (Eds.), *Handbook of reading research, Vol. 3* (pp. 269–84). New York: Longman.

National Center for Education Statistics. (2002). *Schools and staffing survey, 1999–2000: Overview of the data for public, private, public charter, and Bureau of Indian Affairs elementary and secondary schools*. (NCES 2002–313). Washington, DC: U.S. Department of Education, National Center for Educational Statistics.

National Clearinghouse for English Language Acquisition. (2007). *Frequently asked questions*. Retrieved May 15, 2007 from www.ncela.gwu.edu/expert/fastfaq/1.html.

National Institute of Child Health and Human Development. (2000). *Report of the National Reading Panel. Teaching children to read: An evidence-based assessment of the scientific research literature on reading and its implications for reading instruction* (NIH Publication No. 00–4769). Washington, DC: U.S. Government Printing Office.

Oakes, J. (1985). *Keeping track: How schools structure inequality*. New Haven, CT: Yale University Press.

Pajak, E. (2003). *Honoring diverse teaching styles: A guide for supervisors*. Alexandria, VA: Association for Supervision and Curriculum Development.

Parish, T., Merikel, A., Perez, M., Linquanti, R., Socias, M., Spain, M., et al. (2006). *Effects of the implementation of Proposition 227 on the education of English learners, K-12: Findings from a five-year evaluation*. Palo Alto, CA: American Institutes for Research.

Perie, M., Grigg, W.S., & Donahue, P.L. (2005). *The nation's report card: Reading 2005* (NCES 2006–451). National Center for Educational Statistics, U.S. Department of Education. Washington, DC: Government Printing Office.

Phinney, J., Romero, L., Nava, M., & Huang, D. (2001). The role of language, parents and peers in ethnic identity among adolescents in immigrant families. *Journal of Youth and Adolescence, 30*, 135–153.

Saunders, W., & Goldenberg, C. (2001). Strengthening the transition in transitional bilingual education. In D. Christian, & F. Genesee (Eds.), *Bilingual education* (pp. 41–56). Alexandria, VA: TESOL.

Schmoker, M. (1999). *Results: The key to continuous school improvement*. 2nd ed. Alexandria, VA: Association for Supervision and Curriculum Development.

Sherris, A. (2007). The lay of the land: Characteristics of SIOP coaching. In A. Sherris, T. Bauder, & L. Hillyard, *An insider's guide to SIOP coaching* (pp. 3–12). Washington, DC: Center for Applied Linguistics.

Short, D.J. (2002). Language learning in sheltered social studies classes. *TESOL Journal 11*(1), 18–24.

Short, D., & Bauder, T. (2006, May). *Research on SIOP professional development: Year 1 findings*. Paper presented at the NJTESOL/BE Conference.

Short, D.J., & Echevarria, J. (1999). *The sheltered instruction observation protocol: Teacher-researcher collaboration and professional development*. Educational Practice Report No. 3. Santa Cruz, CA and Washington, DC: Center for Research on Education, Diversity & Excellence.

Short, D., & Echevarria, J. (2004/2005). Teacher skills to support English language learners. *Educational Leadership, 62*(4), 8–13.

Short, D., & Fitzsimmons, S. (2007). *Double the work: Challenges and solutions to acquiring language and academic literacy for adolescent English language learners*. Report to Carnegie Corporation of New York. Washington, DC: Alliance for Excellent Education. (http://www.all4ed.org/publications/DoubleWork/index.html).

Siegel, H. (2002). Multiculturalism, universalism, and science education: In search of common ground. *Science Education, 86*, 803–820.

Snyder, T., Dillow, S., & Hoffman, C. (2007). *Digest of Education Statistics, 2006* (NCES 2007–017). Report to the National Center for Educational Statistics, U.S. Department of Education. Washington, DC: Government Printing Office.

Stahl, S. (1999). The cognitive foundations of learning to read: A framework. *Vocabulary development*. Cambridge: Brookline Books.

Tellez, K., & Waxman, H. (2006). A meta-synthesis of qualitative research. In J. Norris, & L. Ortega (Eds.). *Synthesizing Research on Language Learning and Teaching* (pp. 245–277). Philadelphia: John Benjamins Publishing Company.

Thomas, W.P., & Collier, V.P. (2002). *A national study of school effectiveness for language minority students' long-term academic achievement*. Santa Cruz and Washington, DC: Center on Research, Diversity & Excellence.

Toll, C. (2005). *The literacy coach's survival guide: Essential questions and practical answers*. Newark, DE: International Reading Association.

Wong, H. (Winter, 2003). Induction programs that keep working. *Keeping Good Teachers*. Association of Supervision and Curriculum Development.

Vogt, M.E., & Echevarria, J. (2008). *99 ideas and activities for teaching English learners with the SIOP® Model*. Boston: Allyn & Bacon.

Vogt, M.E., & Shearer, B. A. (2007). *Reading specialists and literacy coaches in the real world*. 2nd Ed. Boston: Allyn & Bacon.

Zadina, J. (2004). *Brain research-based effective strategies to enhance learning and energize instruction*. Paper presented at the U.S. Department of Education, Office of English Language Acquisition Summit, Washington, DC, December, 2004.

index